The SPECIALTY SHOP

The SPECIALTY SHOP

How to Create Your Own Unique

and Profitable Retail Business

Dorothy Finell

AMACOM

AMERICAN MANAGEMENT ASSOCIATION
New York * Atlanta * Brussels * Chicago * Mexico City * San Francisco
Shanghai * Tokyo * Toronto * Washington, D.C.

This publication is designed to provide accurate and authoritative information in regard to the subject matter covered. It is sold with the understanding that the publisher is not engaged in rendering legal, accounting, or other professional service. If legal advice or other expert assistance is required, the services of a competent professional person should be sought.

Library of Congress Cataloging-in-Publication Data

Finell, Dorothy.
    The specialty shop : how to create your own unique and profitable retail business / Dorothy Finell.—1st ed.
        p.   cm.
    Includes index.
    ISBN-13: 978-0-8144-7442-6
    ISBN-10: 0-8144-7442-X
    1. Retail trade—Management.   2. New business enterprises.   I. Title.

HF5429.F497   2007
658.8'7—dc22   *2006038832*

Printing number

10   9   8   7   6   5   4   3

Contents

A Stone-Faced Customer   x

Acknowledgments   xii

Introduction   1

1   Planning Your Business   5

Finding Your Niche   6

Furnishings and Apparel   10

Trade Shows and Gift Fairs   11

Financial Planning   15

Success Stories: 17

    The Tea House, *Teas & Accessories*   17

    Every Little Thing, *Miniatures & Collectibles*   20

    Whittaker's, *Gifts*   20

2   Ambience, Décor, and Display   23

Ambience   23

Interior Décor   25

Establishing a Theme 26

Exterior Décor 28

Merchandise Display 30

Vignettes 33

Display Windows 34

Success Stories: 35

La Conversation, *Bakery & Cafe* 35

Buosi, *Men's Apparel* 40

Jan de Luz, *Linens & Furniture* 43

Papier Mâché, *Masks* 45

3 Location, Location, Location 49

Demographics 50

What Not to Look For 52

Carmel, California 52

Success Stories: 56

Helia's, *Women's Apparel* 56

Candlesticks of Carmel, *Candles* 59

Bittner, *Pens & Accoutrements* 61

Cottage of Sweets, *Candies* 61

Nature's Bounty by the Sea, *Gems & Minerals* 64

4 Creating Mini-Boutiques 65

Success Stories: 65

Landis General Store, *Mini-Boutiques & Gifts* 65

Why Not, *Children's Apparel & Toys* 72

KRML, *Radio Station, Retail, Concert Venue* 74

5 Finances   77

   SCORE Advice   77
   Inventory Control   81
   Licenses, Trademarks, Zoning, and Insurance   82
   Taxes   82
   Gaspar Cardinale: Consultant   84
   Success Stories: 89
       The Carmel Hat Company, *Hats*   89
       Henning's, *Cakes & Party Goods*   92

6 Customer Service and Hiring and Training
   Personnel   97

   The Primary Principles of Retailing   98
   Learning the Ropes   99
   Are You In the Right Business?   99
   Hiring   101
   Training   104
   Return Policies   110
   Success Stories: 113
       Husk, *Women's Apparel, Arts & Crafts*   113
       Felloni, *Fabric, Men's Apparel*   117
       Coffee and The Works, *Kitchenware*   120
       Velo Pro and Trailhead, *Bicycles, Camping, Hiking* 123

7 Marketing, Advertising, and Promoting   127

   Defining Marketing   127
   Paid Advertising   129

Newspapers 129

Special-Interest Publications 130

Cable TV 132

Phone Books 133

Put Yourself in the Movies 133

Websites: Individual, Co-op, and E-Commerce 134

Public Relations 138

Newsletters 138

E-Mail Promotions 139

Press Releases 139

Flyers 140

Writing Feature Articles 141

Customized Logos 142

Promotions 142

In-Store Promotions 144

Theater and Other Event Advertising 144

Charity Benefits 145

Gift Wrapping 145

The Best Marketing 146

Success Stories: 147

Scabass, *Women's Apparel* 147

The Book Den, *Secondhand Books* 151

L'Atelier, *Knitting* 154

The Carmel Doll Shop, *Dolls* 157

Juel, *Jewelry* 159

8 Bringing the Community Inside 163

Success Stories: 163

Pilgrim's Way, *Alternative Books* 163

Bella and Daisy's, *Dog Bakery & Accoutrements* 166

Thunderbird Bookshop, *New Books & Gifts* 171

9 Your Grand Opening 175

Invitations 176
Displays 178
Entertainment 178
Giveaways 179
Prizes 180
Refreshments 181
Guest Book 181
Promoting the Grand Opening 182
A Bridal Shop Opening 183
A Shocking Display 184

Appendix A: Trade and Gift Shows 187
Appendix B: E-Commerce Sites 209
Appendix C: Resource Guide to the Success Stories 211
Index 217

A Stone-Faced Customer

One Sunday morning in 1983, the day before we were having the grand opening of the store, we were still working inside the shop, nailing and tacking, although the window displays were done, when a really scruffy, disheveled-looking man with wild hair, unshaven, and wearing torn blue jeans, walked in, pointed to an ensemble in the window and said, "I'll take that. I need size 8 and that looks like it." He didn't even ask the price! It was about $900, I think. Anyway, I was new to the business and nervous, and this was the first customer. I told him it wasn't size 8 and went to look for one. Meanwhile, I was thinking that the man didn't look like he could afford anything, and how was I going to handle this? As it turned out, he had been right and the outfit in the window was size 8. I asked him if he had a credit card, which, to my relief, he produced, and told me that he knew his wife would really like the outfit. I asked him for his address. He said, "Here or in London?" London? So I said both, which he gave me. By this time I was really mystified. Then I asked for his phone number. Again he said, "Here or in London?" Again, I took both, and he told me to send the package to his London address because his wife was there, and he was doing a concert here. A concert? I looked at his name and certainly had never heard of him. So when I got home that night, I asked my son, "Did you ever hear of a Mick Jagger?"

—Mariam Heydari
    Helia's, Washington, D.C.

Acknowledgments

My most heartfelt thanks to Hollie Davies, who was there for me when I really needed her and became an integral part of this book. I am indebted to her.

Also, warm thanks to Patricia Hamilton who inspired me with the idea for the book and to Adrienne Hickey, editor-in-chief, who conveyed to me her enthusiasm from the time she first read it.

To Emily Jordan, my very grateful thanks and warm thanks also to Nancy Fasulo for her participation at the start of this venture.

For his constant encouragement, my loving thanks to Dr. Will Smith who kept me in great condition throughout the writing of this book (and beyond).

My thanks to my marvelous copyeditor, Tina Orem, from whom I learned so much, and to Ali Miner and Pat Matuszewski for their greatly appreciated help. My thanks also to Ann Scott Holt, Andrew Lieberman, Robert Lieberman, and Alex Obert for their help.

Finally, to my friends and others to whom I'm so grateful, thank you: Nadine Smith, Betty Meyer, Pat Mueller-Vollmer, Alan Finell, Michael Weber, Diana Balesteri, Dr. Diana Case, and, of course, Betty McGuire. And last, but certainly not least, my thanks and appreciation to all the shop owners and managers who gave so graciously of their valuable time and knowledge for the interviews.

Census Bureau Statistics[1]

> ➤ About 1.8 million shops start up yearly with only the owner(s); an additional 75,000 open with one employee.

> ➤ Around 587,000 shops with up to four employees go out of business yearly.

> ➤ Approximately 900,000 shops are owned by women, with and without employees.

> ➤ About 1,126,000 small retail shops have up to four employees.

[1]United States Census Bureau (as of 2002, their latest statistics)

Introduction

An estimated 85 percent of new shops close within five years. That means only 15 percent will be successful. The 85 percent of hardworking people who didn't make it have experienced incalculable disappointment, frustration, bankruptcy, and in some cases a loss of life savings or marriages.

As I've walked around my own town's shops over the years, I've been saddened to see how many opened and soon failed; the turnover rate is appalling. And yet, after years as a successful retailer myself, I had already predicted for myself which ones would make it and which ones would fail, simply by visiting these stores a few times. It saddened me so much, particularly because many of these shop owners were young people with a strong desire to succeed. So when my publisher suggested I write a book on the subject, it prompted me to share my many years of retail experience with others and to also include wonderful ideas, innovations, and advice from dozens of other highly successful shop owners in the U.S. and around the world—real shop owners with expert experience to share with you. Their sensitive and thoughtful advice will fire up your imagination and humanize the process of starting a business by balancing the business side with your creative side.

As you will see, ideas that work for one shop owner don't necessarily work for another, and you will understand why as you read the descriptions of the owners' shops and how they got started. Some have the most exquisite display windows I've ever seen; others have none at all. Some advertise heavily in local papers, but many do no advertising at all, preferring public relations events to attract new customers. Yet all are successful using creative methods they've developed based upon their own needs.

My goal is to help you achieve *your* goal of being one of the 15 percent who make it, or if you are already in business and struggling, to transform your business into one that will remain successful for many years to come. And, of course, I want to help you avoid costly mistakes that can turn your dreams into nightmares.

The information provided in the Success Stories relates to all types of shops and niche markets, but I paid special attention to the following categories because the shops in this book include them as main inventory categories or subcategories. These are some of the categories you might want to choose from for your own niche, and there are many others in the book.

Men's apparel (and accessories)

Women's apparel (and accessories)

Children's apparel and toys (and accessories)

Camping and hiking (and accessories)

Bicycle (and accessories)

Linens (and related items)

Coffee (and related items)

Knitting yarns (and related items)

Masks (and related items)

Hats

Notions

Business and art supplies

Pets (and accessories)

Jewelry

Bakeries and cafés (and related items)

Tea (and related items)

Stationery and cards

Books

Shoes (and accessories)

Fabrics (and related items)

Kitchen and housewares (and related items)

Paper goods, wrapping paper, and ribbons

Gifts

Frames

China

Lamps

Glassware

Silver

Skin and beauty products

Collectibles

Travel

The areas of advice in this book include:

➤ Planning and researching your niche business.

➤ Choosing a successful location.

➤ General planning and merchandise.

➤ Ambience, décor, and display.

➤ Working with buying offices.

➤ Finances.

➤ Hiring, training, and keeping good personnel.

➤ Advertising, events, and special promotions.

➤ Personal advice and ideas from successful specialty-shop owners around the world. Thirty existing shops are featured, and 32 specialty shop owners were interviewed for the book.

I studied and analyzed many niche shops, but I chose the shops included here based on my own criteria of excellence. They are the best examples in Los Angeles, California; West Hartford, Connecticut; Paris, France; several locations in Italy; London, England; Carmel, California; and a number of cities in Australia, among them Sydney, Melbourne, and Canberra. I carefully inspected these shops, interviewed their owners, and further analyzed how other shopkeepers—collectively in a city or town—rated their displays, décor, and personnel. Each of these shops sells one or more types of niche merchandise or is a niche business itself. I was not interested in operations that spent ridiculous amounts of money in order to be beautiful. I chose *fascinating, imaginative, creative, extraordinary shops with a remarkable ambience*—this is the essence of an outstanding niche shop.

It is the unique individuality of décor, display, merchandise, personnel, and, of course, longevity—the complete combination—that rates a shop as extraordinary by my standards. In Italy, for example, where I visited eight towns or small cities, the three extraordinary businesses written up here met all of my specifications for an outstanding shop, whereas in well-known areas of major cities where I *expected* to find a host of good examples, I found not a single one that fit all of my criteria!

It was humanly impossible, of course, to see every shop in the United States, Europe, or Australia. And there will undoubtedly be other shops in the geographic areas I chose that are successful but are not included.

If you feel your niche shop is exceptional and fits the criteria I have used, please let me know. We might include it in a future book on niche shops. You can e-mail me at dorfin9255@aol.com.

Chapter 1

Planning Your Business

The benefits of owning a niche shop are many. Retailers worldwide have told me time and again that a single category or a one-product line—a retail niche business—is appealing because it is safer, more cost efficient, and less wasteful because there are fewer markdowns. But to be successful, you must distinguish your chosen niche business as a niche operation and nothing else. Throughout this book you will find dozens of interviews with successful owners of niche shops in the U.S., Europe, and Australia, and their advice is an invaluable source of ideas, encouragement, and secrets of success.

What is a niche? In whole or in part a niche fills a void of some kind. It is popular merchandise (not fads) that other local shops don't carry and that you think customers are looking for. An entire shop can be a niche business, just as one item—in various forms— can be a niche item when it is set apart from the rest of the shop. In fact, in this book you will find several examples of shops that have created as many as 12 mini-boutiques within their shops, all of which are niche boutiques because the merchandise carried in each boutique is different from merchandise in the other boutiques.

With more and more chain stores and shops carrying the same stock, it is imperative in today's market for your retail enterprise to be unique!

Finding Your Niche

Once you've decided to become a retailer, the next step is to decide what categories you might like to carry. Many of the shop owners you will read about chose categories that they personally loved and had great interest in: from pens to used books, wedding cakes to exotic masks, and miniature porcelains to expensive women's and men's apparel. The following categories will give you an idea of the wide range to choose from, and there are many more. When you visit trade shows and gift shows, you will be overwhelmed by the wonderful choices available to you. Information about the leading trade and gift shows, as well as "buying offices" for apparel, appears in appendix A.

Categories

Albums & Scrapbooks
Antiques
Antique Reproductions
Apparel
Baby Items
Balloons
Barware
Baskets, Wicker

Bath & Boudoir Accessories
Beach Accessories
Books & Publications
Brassware, Bronze &
    Accessories
Bridal Accessories
Calendars
Candles & Candlesticks

Candy
Ceramics
Christmas Decorations
Clocks, Watches
Collectibles
Country Crafts
Crafts, Contemporary
Crafts, Traditional
Crystal
Custom or Private-Label Work
Decorative Pillows &
    Tapestries
Desk Accessories, Letter
    Openers
Dinnerware
Display Fixtures,
    Equipment & Supplies
Dolls
Educational Items
Electronics & Gadgets
Environmental Products
Ethnic Artifacts & Folk Art
Fashion Accessories
Figurines
Flatware, Cutlery
Floor Coverings & Rugs
Florist Accessories & Planters
Flowers, Artificial & Dried
Furniture
Games, Puzzles, Playing Cards
Garden Accessories

Gift Bags
Gift Boxes
Gift Wrap & Ribbons
Glassware
Gourmet Foods
Greeting Cards
Hobby Merchandise
Holloware
Home Entertaining
Home Textiles, Rugs &
    Throws
Housewares Accessories
Ice Buckets & Coasters
Jewelry Boxes
Jewelry, Fashion
Jewelry, Fine
Kaleidoscopes
Kitchen Textiles &
    Accessories
Leather Goods & Luggage
Lighting
Linens, Bedding, Pillows
Memorabilia
Men's Gifts
Miniatures
Mobiles
Mugs
Museum Reproductions
Music Boxes
Musical Gifts
Nautical Gifts

Novelties & Impulse Items

Office Products & Supplies

Paperweights

Party Goods

Patriotic Gifts

Pens & Writing Instruments

Perfume Bottles

Personal Care Items

Pet Items

Pewter

Placemats

After you choose your main category, you need to create an in-depth plan that addresses what types of accessories would go well with your choice. If you choose men's apparel, for example, besides the basic categories of pants, sportswear, and shirts, will you also carry underwear, socks, belts, shoes, ties, or ascots? Will your shirts be formal or casual, or a mix of both? What sizes will you buy? If you choose a pen shop, will you also carry stationery, diaries, inks, and pen paraphernalia? If you plan to open a jewelry store, will you carry genuine jewels, costume jewelry, or a mix of both? Will you carry items for men, or women, or children, or all three? Ideas for offering accessories or special services to bring customers in are limited only to your own creativity. For example, The Carmel Doll Shop in Carmel, California, offers repair services for dolls, doll-houses, and clothing in addition to selling many beautiful and often rare dolls.

If you open an apparel shop in Florida and specialize exclusively in resort and cruise wear, you might want to add a travel-desk corner that stocks pamphlets, brochures, and related information about resorts in Florida and other states. A travel agent or consultant, employed by the owner, could run the niche operation.

Many years ago when Danskin—a manufacturer of tights, leotards, shorts, tops, and scores of items related to dance and exercise—became incredibly popular with every female in the U.S., my husband and I decided to add a Danskin boutique in each of our stores, which developed into a niche business in itself.

Cookbooks, specialty books, and gift books can also become niches in themselves. Edie Frére, co-owner of Landis General Store, which has 10 niche boutiques within one shop, says that *Tiffany's Table Manners for Teenagers* has become a niche in itself because the book appeals to the particular customers in her upscale Los Angeles location.

If you are in a tourist area, you might want to add niche categories that cater to tourists. For example, if you are located in a historic city with or without a major museum and no other shops carry museum items, you might want to consider such a mini-niche in your own shop. The Boston Gift Show, the San Francisco International Gift Fair, and the New York trade shows all carry museum reproductions, and these could well be good sellers for you. If you live in a university city or town where the population is geared to cultural activities, a cultural niche operation of some kind is a natural tie-in—as long as the prices are also geared to the demographics of such a population.

You can read more about creating mini-boutiques in Chapter 4.

* * *

Underlying all your planning is The Golden Rule: The Right Item, at the Right Time, in the Right Place, at the Right Price. The Golden Rule is the first rule, the cardinal rule—the foundation, in fact, of good retailing.

The right item, of course, will be the one you have chosen and can't wait to sell.

The right time is self-evident. You wouldn't sell swimsuits in a shop in northern Minnesota in January, for instance. Nor would you sell children's ski suits in a Florida store in August. These are blatant examples of when *not* to sell. But a more subtle example is deciding to buy discounted Christmas items at 50 percent off and then selling them in January. At the time, the offer to buy discounted stock seems irresistible. However, it would tie up money needed for the next season's purchases. The right place will be an ideal, well-researched location for your shop, which I discuss in Chapter 3. Of course, there are exceptions to each part of The Golden Rule, including location. (We all know of instances where a shop is located in the middle of nowhere and it has no trouble thriving. But those are rare exceptions.)

> **tip**
>
> One obvious but often neglected tip: carry a notebook with you at all times as you plan your business. Write down everything that could be of importance to you later on. If you see a window display that appeals to your taste, make a note of what it is you like about it. If shop owners are kind enough to help you, take notes on what they tell you. And, of course, keep track of what other shops carry so that you won't be carrying exactly the same items in the same area.

The right price will be a product of your financial planning, your visits to trade shows, and your pricing research.

Furnishings and Apparel

Generally speaking, the two most common classifications of merchandise found in shops are home or office furnishings and apparel.

A word of explanation is in order about the difference between shops and stores. A furniture *shop* might carry a few pieces of furniture, and perhaps sell its display items. But a furniture shop does not carry a full line of furniture—that is, every piece for every room of a house. That is the purpose of a furniture *store* which, by defini-tion is of very large or huge proportion. The same holds true for department stores, such as Macy's, Sears, or Bloomingdale's. They have furniture departments that cater to certain rooms of a house or an office, but they are not furniture stores.

Home furnishings is a catch-all term for furnishings found both within the home as well as the exterior—or "home and garden," as it's commonly called. This category is common at gift shows, and it excludes specialties such as sporting equipment, which is usually found in stores, not shops. Other trade shows cater to those special-ties.

Trade Shows and Gift Fairs

To see and become familiar with the incredible choices for your shop, you need to visit a trade show or gift fair. Your first trip to the trade shows will probably be for research and as a study tool, rather than as an actual first-time buyer. As you walk along the aisles of the show, jot down all the ideas that come to mind as a result of what you've seen—all the specific items you would like to carry in addition to the general categories.

tip

At some shows—and this is very important if you are in the plan-ning stage—a new-buyer orien-tation is one of several lectures/ seminars offered, and you should plan on attending.

Each show you attend will present items and ideas or even a new product line that could create a niche for you or, at the least, add to your existing merchandise categories.

The categories encompassed within the world of gift shows are many and varied. So if you're planning to open a shop that sells any sort of furnishings for the home, for instance, you'll not only want to attend your regional gift show but the New York International Gift Fair (NYIGF) as well. In fact, attendance at the latter show is mandatory, I strongly believe. You'll see almost everything your competition carries and thousands more items besides.

The NYIGF always takes place in the city at the end of January and lasts a week. Plan to spend several days there if you are in the planning stage, and a week if you have progressed to the buying stage. The NYIGF covers the following areas:

➤ Home—furniture, lighting, floor coverings, art, textiles, bath and home accessories

➤ Floral and garden—outdoor furniture, silk and dried flowers, vases, garden kits and supplies, baskets, ribbons, ornaments

➤ General gift—stationery, collectibles, ceramic giftware, pottery, toys, pet items, party trend merchandise, souvenirs and novelties, specialty foods, general import items, Christmas decorations

➤ Children—educational products, toys, games, puzzles, gifts, apparel, books, bedding, stuffed toys, furniture, and accessories

➤ Personalized accessories—Fashion accessories, jewelry, handbags, men's gifts, aromatherapy, apparel

➤ Tabletop and housewares—bakeware, barware, china, cookware, cutlery/flatware, dinnerware, electrics, gadgets, glassware, kitchenware, table linens, bed and bath linens, kitchen textiles, and decorative tabletop items

➤ Miscellaneous—books, calendars, novelties, ethnic and folk-art items, historical products, Judaica, posters, jewelry, and art pieces

➤ Handmade—many categories of above

➤ Antiques

There is another NYIGF every August, though it is not as large or as complete as January's. Other gift shows are listed in Appendix A to give you an idea of how many shows there are and in what areas. For an updated list of shows, go to www.nyigf.com or www .biztradeshows.com.

Study the items at the NYGIF shows very carefully for they are the most complete trade shows in the country. But also attend your regional show because it may carry regional items that the New York shows don't. For example, the Boston Gift Show in March carries a made-in-New-England category that might well provide you with an exclusive item or two. Perhaps—if you're the first person to see it—you'll have the whole line to yourself, particularly if you live in a town or small city. It's certainly worth discussing with the line's sales representative.

While at any trade show, even for study purposes, as you walk from one resource to another in which you're interested, ask the sales representative (or "rep," as they're known) for brochures, lists, and videos of everything they have. You may *think* you'll remember everything, but take it from one who learned the hard way. By the time you arrive home, you'll remember almost nothing; your mind will be overloaded. So pick their brains. Ask them every question you can possibly think of—you'd be surprised how eager they are to inform you of their products and how helpful they'll be when they know you're planning to open a shop. In fact, some reps will be overeager, sometimes to the point of being pushy. They try to get their products into your store once they've determined that you are right for their resource (read "right" as financially solvent), so let that be a word of caution!

As for the apparel market—which includes accessories and shoes—the trade shows for buyers are broken down by regions and, in turn, the cities that best represent those regions. Although there are other shows in smaller cities, I've chosen to list only the major markets in appendix A because the greatest number of manufacturers show their merchandise in those cities.

The value of the apparel trade shows lies in the fact that they can provide you with all the resources you want and need. After you see a show, you can proceed to the showrooms of each of your favored resources to view their whole lines. If you wish, the salesperson can write up your order right then, or you can go home and mail or e-mail the rep at a later time with your order. What's good about viewing the entire line at the showroom is that it enables you to find the one perfect item that you would never have seen because you wouldn't have thought of or known about it. (But, you wouldn't have bothered to go to a showroom for just one thing anyway.) Your time is generally too valuable in the market to spend the extra hour just looking. Though, to keep up with trends, if you're going the trade-show-and-showroom route, it is necessary to do so a few times a year.

There are twice as many shows for womenswear as menswear—which is in keeping with the number of shops countrywide for each of those two categories. The children's market is often represented in conjunction with the womenswear shows as well as in shows that represent all three categories. There are two huge childrenswear shows, which is why, I think, there are so few trade shows for them alone.

Appendix A lists shows by month. Some shows may be cancelled or moved for various reasons, so for current schedules and information check www.biztradeshows.com or www.nyigf.com.

If all of your planning indicates that your choice of a niche category (or categories) is a good one with no competition and lots of potential customers, then you know you have a winner.

Financial Planning

In Chapter 5 you will find information about financing, which will be more relevant when you are ready to raise capital for your business. But before you reach that stage you will need a preliminary estimate of the costs of your new enterprise. The easiest way to introduce yourself to this type of financial overview—one that you will need in order to secure a loan—is to download forms from the Service Corps of Retired Executives (SCORE) website (www.score .org). SCORE is a resource partner with the Small Business Administration (SBA) and its services are free. Downloadable forms include:

➤ Business Plan for a Start-Up Business

➤ Business Plan for an Established Business

➤ Balance Sheet (Projected)

➤ Bank Loan Request for Small Business

➤ Breakeven Analysis

➤ Cash Flow Statement (12 Months)

➤ Competitive Analysis

➤ Financial History & Ratios

➤ Loan Amortization Schedule

➤ Nondisclosure Agreement

➤ Opening Day Balance Sheet

➤ Personal Financial Statement

➤ Profit and Loss Projection (12 Months)

➤ Profit and Loss Projection (Three Years)

➤ Sales Forecast (12 Months)

➤ Start-Up Expenses

In addition to downloading forms, you can ask a SCORE counselor to review your business plan with you. You can also attend SCORE's free small-business seminars. A SCORE planning course includes information about business plans, necessary financing, taxes, licenses, permits, bookkeeping, and start-up costs.

Success Stories

The Tea House is an exquisite niche shop in London, England, one of the world's great shopping meccas. Competition is fierce.

The owner of The Tea House, Christina Smith, emphasized to me that her shop is a niche business because she is a "specialist in fine teas, infusions, and teaphernalia," which also happens to be the motto of the shop. "Teaphernalia" is an outgrowth of the tea import company that she started in 1963 when she journeyed to China twice a year for 18 years. In 1981 she decided to open a shop that today is located in the chic, bustling Covent Garden area of London—a very fashionable and artistic section of shops and theatres in a jammed-with-tourists district.

For a total of 911 square feet, 500 of it as main-floor selling space and 411 of ground-floor footage that includes a small storage area, Christina pays an exorbitant amount of rent and taxes because of the shop's location. So she uses a warehouse that costs a fractional amount to house the huge amounts of tea she stocks. A member of her staff goes once or twice weekly to resupply the many different varieties.

Strictly a tea shop (no coffee, candies, or such), The Tea House nonetheless carries 24 types of marmalade as accompaniments for scones, different kinds of honey for tea, infusers, teapots, and tea tins for storage. Altogether, Christina carries almost 150 types of tea that break down as follows:

> *Black Tea:* Eleven traditional blends including six in teabags, five kinds from Ceylon, 10 types from India, six from China (this includes 10 types in teabag form), and seven from other countries

- ➤ **_Flavored Black Tea:_** Twenty-eight types in both loose and teabag form, in flavors such as mango, lychee, passion fruit, tropical fruit, blood orange, black currant, apricot ginger, ginseng, chocolate truffle, rum, caramel, Indian chai spice, coconut, licorice, almond, and others

- ➤ **_Caffeine-Free Infusions:_** Eight kinds of whole-fruit blends and 16 of herbs and flowers (including at least three in teabag form), such as kir royale, summer pudding, Christmas pudding, fennel seed mix, hibiscus flowers, and raspberry leaves

- ➤ **_Green Tea:_** Sixteen kinds from China (three in teabag form) and six from Japan

- ➤ **_Flavored Green Tea:_** Japanese-style grown in China, flavors such as vanilla, kiwi, strawberry, green cherry, and wild cherry

- ➤ **_Rooibos:_** Six kinds, including one in teabag form

The story of rooibos, Christina told me, is fascinating. _Rooibos_, which means "red bush," is mentioned in the current popular book series _The No. 1 Ladies' Detective Agency_ by Alexander McCall Smith. Locals, tourists, and mail-order customers are creating a great demand for it, thanks to the book!

The Tea House sells 53 percent of its tea under its own label. The shop sends the most popular types to a teabag maker.

About 58 percent of the shop's customers are tourists from the European Union, about 38 percent are from the United Kingdom, and the rest are Japanese and other foreigners. The Tea House does a small mail-order business—small because orders are taken through fax, mail, and phone—Smith does not own a computer.

As for teapots, the sheer numbers, variety, styles, and colors are astonishing and has created another niche for Christina. There are new ones, antique ones, and one-of-a-kinds. In fact, it was the display of teapots in the windows that first inspired me to look inside and see what the shop was all about. Displayed as window boxes, with each teapot representing England or other countries or events, they draw onlookers like flies—most of them, like me, wanting to see more inside. There I found six different designs of London novelty teapots in various sizes, 15 different designs of other novelty kinds, an English traditional teapot in eight colors, three Chinese pots in ten different patterns and different shapes, Japanese teapots in three sizes and one color, and 12 different designs of Japanese tea sets. All this, as well as English tea sets and 12 different patterns of one-person tea sets!

Overall, Christina informed me, the same number of customers exist today as a few years ago, but people are spending less—the "Golden Era" of sales was the 1980s.

Asked to share her secret of success, she replied, "Staying small." And her greatest assets? "Tenacity, perseverance, and honesty." Her advice: "Don't copy someone else's operation. Create a true niche business. Get practical experience in the same specialized business that you want to open."

I have seen many tea shops in England and around the world, but none more intriguing than the ambience of The Tea Shop, which fairly shouts, "We sell only tea—smell it!" It's marvelously exotic yet quintessentially British—the kind of shop where just as many men shop as women and everybody wants to buy something, including me.

*   *   *

Every Little Thing, in Carmel, California, is not only a gift shop, it's a collectors' paradise. In a 625-square-foot shop, owner Kaki Richardson stocks 49 categories of collectibles, of which 11 collections are miniatures, including people, animals, shoes, cups, tea sets, teapots, Raggedy Annes, cottages, boxes, cars, thimbles, vegetables, and fruits. Even the "taller" collectibles are no more than 10 inches high. Collections come in various materials such as ceramic, metal, wood, or cloth.

The abundance of collections as well as the abundance of individual items within each collection is especially important because customers are searching for what they don't have—the one or two items new to them. This necessitates a huge stock of merchandise.

Kaki has owned this business for 15 years and says her location is so superb that she doesn't need to advertise. Word-of-mouth and foot traffic are her best advertising. Her customers are 60 percent tourists and 40 percent locals. What she saves on advertising allows her to purchase more merchandise.

Trade shows are very important to her, and she attends five or six each year around the U.S. She might find a whole new group of collectibles that she will want to stock, perhaps miniature dolls or buildings of a particular era, or train cars, for example. She might find different types of shoes or boxes or animals made by a new manufacturer, or a new country or state that was never represented before. A category such as boxes, which were previously only made of pottery or china, may show up made of wood. She might also find just one new item that she can add to a collection she already has.

* * *

Whittaker's, in Carmel, California, combines an art gallery with home furnishings. The owner, Willa Aylaian, is an artist herself, and her displays, both window and interior, reflect that with their eye-catching charm. The shop's location couldn't be more advantageous—near Carmel's major hotels, inns, and other retail establishments. Within its 800-square-foot interior, Willa mixes hand-painted pottery, dinnerware, tabletop objects, table linens, wildflowers, baskets, an eclectic mix of furniture, and anything else she believes will sell to her many repeat customers. The artistic way in which Willa displays her stock creates a warm, homelike ambience.

She told me her major secret (one that defies the popular advice of always reordering a hot item): she never reorders the same thing. She maintains a fresh, new, different look by always buying new items and even new categories, thereby turning merchandise over quickly and satisfying repeat customers.

Chapter 2

Ambience, Décor, and Display

Ambience, interior and exterior décor, merchandise display, and display windows are all intricately intertwined and cannot be separated. In this chapter, you'll see how each element interplays with the others to create the full and unique personality of your shop.

Ambience

Think of ambience as a combination of all that your customers see, hear, feel, and smell when they visit your shop: from the exterior landscaping, decorating, and signage, to your display windows, to the interior of your shop—including the look and feel of the color scheme, paint, woods or other materials, display cases, shelving, and merchandise displays. All of these elements reflect your personality and the personality of your shop. Over time a shop develops an ambience all its own, and this will be important to your overall success.

Activities inside your store can also add to ambience. If you establish certain types of sales and promotions that become well-known and anticipated, that alone is part of ambience. It's what people come to expect of you.

The first year that I owned *The Gazebo* I dreamt up an innovation at Christmas time—Men's Night—which took place on a weeknight after business hours. I sent out handwritten invitations to men whose girlfriends or wives were our customers. We poured drinks for the men and catered to them further by modeling the clothes if they were interested in a specific item. One or two of my preteen daughters, who earned extra money for their "jobs," gift wrapped their packages in special paper and ribbon that we used only for men's gifts. The wrapping in itself became a status symbol in ensuing years. So many men came, bringing friends, that eventually Men's Night became *the* place to shop during the Christmas season. It was a raving success!

Another idea that became popular and added to our overall ambience was that twice a year in all of our stores we organized a spectacular, end-of-season Very Last Day Sale with 50 to 70 percent discounts. This was almost unheard of in those days. We also held a sidewalk sale in July.

It is a compliment to you as an owner if repeat customers and potential customers in your area look forward to and depend on your traditions, whether they are regular sales, special events, or other promotional ideas.

Interior Décor

There are three types of displays: interior, exterior, and windows, and each of these generally involves three parts—basic equipment, display props, and display materials. The basis of display equipment includes shelving, racks, and showcases. You can use the usual, boring, everyone-has-them type of equipment, or you can search at auctions and second-hand shops for the unusual—pieces that have a distinct style that further enhances your theme and adds to the ambience of your shop. You can also design and construct your own shelving and racks that will tie into your theme. If shelves constructed of wood appear to be an armoire, for instance, you've automatically created a different look. If racks are of early twentieth-century construction, either antiques or reproductions, again you've

Items brought in from home create an elegant display area at Jan de Luz in Carmel, California.

added an outstanding touch. And if you've utilized all sorts of old and interesting tables to showcase a category of merchandise, you've also added to the ambience in addition to creating an interesting way to display stock.

Display props consist of mannequins, furniture, sports equipment, garden, household, or office furnishings. In other words, just about anything. But again, tie them to your overall theme and scheme. Look through everything in your own home, from pictures to kitchenware to furniture to tools, to see if anything you already own can be used for displays. Do you have a long mirror? Old and interesting tools? A collection of something that might look great in a window with merchandise surrounding it? How about a beat-up old chest that could feature lots of stock items tumbling from it? A lovely vase from which to hang necklaces? When you use antiques as props, a table, chair, chest, or whatever can tie a window display to the interior and thereby create an integrated whole. It will also save you a lot of money.

Establishing a Theme

A theme is very important to the overall subject of ambience. How imaginative are you? Be creative!

An excellent example of a shop utilizing props to match its theme is **Why Not** in Alexandria, Virginia. Owner Kate Schlabach's enterprise beautifully incorporates props—antique pieces, fitting for a library in such a historic city and refreshingly innovative and uncommon in a children's store. Some of the antiques are unusual in themselves or, as Kate put it, "different" in her utilization of them. Instead of a stepstool, as almost all stores would use, she utilizes a brass-and-wood sliding ladder from an old hardware company to reach items high up, thereby accomplishing two goals at once: she puts the antique to good use and it in turn contributes to the interior ambience. Likewise, the large, floor-to-ceiling wood apothecary cabinet, once at home in a pharmacy, serves two purposes. One half, with many small drawers, creatively displays reproduction tin toys and old books (for example, Kate arranged stuffed rabbits around a book about a rabbit) and is used downstairs; the other half, upstairs, contains Playmobil toys.

Another example, this one in Carmel, California, is **Redeem**. The motto on the store's business card is "Unique and Affordable Home Furnishings," and the shop is just that. Veronica O'Shea, the owner, started with a 500-square-foot space which, five years later, expanded to 1,000 square feet when she acquired the shop next door, creating one spacious, brightly lit establishment. The collection of pillows, lamps, decorative items, small furniture, candles, small fountains, ceramics, serving pieces, utensils, and photographic art is arrayed in a harmonious blend of elegant displays that Veronica creates herself; the ultimate effect is an ambience of serenity that is felt the moment one enters the shop.

Each individual display grouping features items of one color and material blended with subtle accents of another one or two neutral colors, with contrasting materials mixed in. With several displays featuring these dynamic color themes, the whole effect of the shop is nothing short of exciting.

Hermes shops are another example of good prop use. The former saddlery company has incorporated an equine theme in all its displays since the famous company began. It often displays saddles in its windows, and the theme continues in the shop's interior:

antique books about horses, a bridle, stirrups, and Hermes' own colorful signature scarves are just a small part of the related displays.

Display materials not only cast the mood and create the atmosphere, but they also pull together the elements of all the displays—interior, windows, and exterior. Leaves, branches, silk flowers, tubes of suntan lotion, Coke bottles, boxes of cake mix, streamers, and balloons are among the thousands of choices of materials that create seasonal ambience. Autumn leaves tossed here or there in the windows and throughout the shop suggest autumn, just as stems of lavender suggest summer.

A shop in Vermont, for instance, might use a sled, sleigh, ice skates, fake snowballs, snowflakes, a jug of cider, and baskets of apples as props to create a winter theme and ambience. A toy store or children's shop might utilize balloons or schoolbooks in its displays. How about plastic containers of flour and sugar, a bottle of vanilla, and empty containers of butter and eggs laid on a table in the display window of a kitchen shop? There are countless items costing little or nothing that can add to displays inside and out, and cut down on your display budget.

Exterior Décor

The outside of your shop should be eye-catching and welcoming, whether you are a barber shop or an expensive apparel shop, and it should tie in with your niche.

* * *

Outside a barber shop in an upscale town in Connecticut, I found the enthusiastic owner of **West Hartford Professional Family Hair Care**, Tom Reddin, who loves his work and also loves landscaping. Tom created a small garden area on the sidewalk in front of his display window, complete with potted plants surrounding a wooden horse, a park bench, and an old-fashioned barber pole. He changes his horticultural displays with the holidays and seasons and, besides for the fun of it, he says he feels he's "contributing to

and for the look of the street, the town, and the people of West Hartford." People are so intrigued by the creative garden that they enter the shop to say a few words to Tom and then ask if they can look at the museum-like collection. Sometimes they become customers, and that's the point of offering an unusual and interesting exterior—to entice potential customers to come in and browse.

In business 40 years, Tom's shop consisted of plain chairs until a few years ago when he came across some 1950s barber chairs and transformed the whole shop to reflect the

This hair salon attracts customers of all ages with its whimsical exterior displays, including a boat filled with flowers of the season.

1950s look. He collected and hung everything pertaining to Elvis Presley, including all of his eight-inch records, as well as restaurant menus, model cars, and '50s photos of servicemen and the downtown area.

*   *   *

Another example of extending an interior theme to a shop's exterior is **Tiger Lilly Florist**,* in Carmel, California, which opened in 1978 and was acquired by Kyong Morsdome in 1999. She retained the highly experienced manager who joined the business in 1984. Once a service station 40 years ago, the shop is composed of bricks, beams, and a curved archway, reflecting an air of old-world charm. It is well lighted and has several display windows. Kyong incorporated her product into the décor. Numerous varieties of exotic orchids, greenery, out-of-the-ordinary plants and flowers, dried flower arrangements, and wreaths—some of which decorate a large, antique, wrought-iron gazebo—add to the magical ambience of this small shop. Antiques are at home with the store's modern touches, and even with the many unusual planters, baskets, vases, and other accessories, the interior retains an uncluttered, serene appearance, accented by soothing floral scents.

Kyong uses the narrow pedestrian breezeway on the side of the building as exterior promotion for her shop, transforming it into a garden entrance with 15-inch-high animal topiaries and flowering plants hanging from the ceiling or sitting in unusual wicker stands.

Kyong offered this advice to newcomers: "The right location is imperative, but the presentation of displays and quality of merchandise are just as important. If you are acquiring an already-successful business, don't tamper with success!"

Merchandise Display

As customers move around your shop, do they encounter an uncomplicated progression of merchandise from one category to the

---

*Just prior to publication of this book, Jane Bok Kim became the new owner of Tiger Lilly and plans to make no changes to this delightful shop.

next? For instance, do all items pertaining to a bathroom follow, in logical order, bedroom merchandise, which in turn follows the kitchen linens? Or are sheets next to washcloths, which are next to dishcloths, followed by bath towels? This may be an extreme example, perhaps, but I've seen such illogical presentation of stock, especially in apparel shops.

Once you have completed your initial buying, which means you've purchased your display fixtures, including props, shelves, racks, and showcases (or you have the measurements for these items from a catalog or other source prior to buying), you need to estimate how many square feet are required for each category of merchandise. Of course this might seem difficult to accomplish, but it really is not if you follow what I call a Blueprints Plan:

➤ Compose a master list of *all the categories* you plan to carry, and *all the items* of each category. As an example, let's assume you are opening an apparel shop. How many types of tops did you buy? How many bottoms? How many coats? How many jackets? You get the idea.

➤ Now subcategorize these items. How many tops are T-shirts? How many cotton tops? How many silk? How many bottoms are slacks or jeans or shorts? How many types of coats are wool? How many are raincoats? Now breakdown the subcategories into individual styles and sizes of each.

➤ Calculate each subcategory as a percentage of the entire category.

➤ Calculate each category as a percentage of your entire stock.

For the placement of merchandise on shelves, racks, and in display props, estimate:

➤ Which style categories need racks only

➤ Which style categories need shelves only

➤ Which subcategories need shelves and display props such as cabinets, armoires, bookcases, or other

➤ Which subcategories need to be housed within props only, such as a niche category or categories

➤ Which subcategories need glass showcases and props only, such as accessories

➤ Which categories need showcases only, such as jewelry, the cash register, the credit card machine, and wrapping materials

➤ Which subcategories need only hanging space

Study the *exact dimensions* of your shop, both horizontally and vertically, and lay out (on graph paper or a computer) shelves, racks, props, and showcases. Take into account where you will store duplicates of merchandise. Above shelves? Below showcases? In a back room? At home?

Estimate other priorities:

➤ What items need to be placed into the selling space? Where will you fit them in a sales area? What will you need to store? (Usually, storage is in the back, beyond the selling space.)

> ➤ Determine where you will place items that need to be hung, such as belts, ties, scarves, bags, etc.

Add and transfer all of this information onto the drawing. You now have as complete and cohesive a blueprint as possible. Having a blueprint is essential to the smooth startup of your business, and it is fun to see your shop developing, even if it's only on paper or a computer screen. But if you are truly hopeless at this type of planning, have a friend show you how, or take a course. You are going to be in business a long time, and understanding how to plan and rearrange your interior is invaluable. Think of how much easier it will be on move-in day when every item of stock and every piece of heavy equipment carried in has a place. You don't want to be left with a chaos of impossibly heavy equipment surrounding you after the movers have gone and you have the grand opening planned for the next day! Also, having a blueprint enables you to make small but possibly necessary changes to your shop. It enables you to *see* that you have extra usable floor space here, or wall space there, and you can fill it with anything you need.

Vignettes

Vignettes are two or more items that tell a little story. Displayed on a glass showcase, a shelf, cabinet, bookcase, on a lovely prop, hanging, or even on the floor, they evoke an image, an impression, or a visual scene. The purpose of vignettes is not only to showcase the items themselves but also to portray a coordinated ensemble which, hopefully, a customer will buy in its entirety.

Moving and changing merchandise and displays around are

particularly important in the gift, home furnishings, and apparel fields because it is not unusual for customers to miss seeing items placed in high or low places. Remember that a customer's eyes tend to look straight ahead and slightly above and below, but for various reasons they seldom view what is very high or very low. With this knowledge in mind, you can understand the philosophy of frequently moving and changing the stock from one place to another. And every few days, feature a different display at the front of the shop.

Display Windows

This is one area where imagination and ideas are limitless. One of the more memorable displays I remember was a urinal in a glitzy Las Vegas china-and-crystal gift shop. The urinal was filled with wine, and above it was an antique display cabinet with graduated shelves, which housed every size wine goblet imaginable. Not everyone's taste, perhaps, but it certainly attracted many people to the shop. Along the same lines, in a Springfield, Massachusetts, garden shop, a gold-handled urinal held a spectacular display of flowers that was being delivered to a wedding reception.

Outside an Aspen, Colorado, young men's shop, I saw a male mannequin dressed in sweats, sneakers, and bicycle helmet. He sat atop a bicycle that seemed as if it were about to crash through the display window. Another male mannequin, elegantly dressed, stood next to a female mannequin wearing only a short ski jacket and knee-hi socks. The display was imaginative and startling.

I also once saw a very realistic sculpture (probably by Seward Johnson) of a man holding a ladder and paint brush in front of the window of a gift shop in Santa Barbara. The sculpture caused everyone to stop and look, and I noticed several went into the shop.

When my husband and I owned The Gazebo, I had a window designer for some years, but as I became more creative with displays I began to do them myself—as I did with the feature displays on either side of the front door. I used antiques, including a captain's chest, a chair, a small table, and whatever I could spare from our house as props. I incorporated whatever was the hot item at the time with costume jewelry and purses, scarves, and various accessories such as pajamas and teddy bears (those were a hot item during the early seventies), piled on, in, or around the antiques. My husband and older sons also brought me an armoire from our house because it had a large mirror attached to it and many drawers. I placed a mannequin standing in front of the mirror with all sorts of apparel and accessories falling out of the drawers. It was very innovative at that time and very effective. It caught the eyes of onlookers who hadn't previously noticed that we existed and brought them into The Gazebo where, thereafter, they frequently made purchases. The displays acted as the setting for the overall ambience of the shop—just as the smaller interior displays furthered that theme and ambience.

Success Stories

The following are all examples of wonderful niche shops that rated very highly in my criteria for inclusion in this book, and especially high for ambience, décor, and display.

La Conversation, a delectable French bakery and café in California, is an outstanding example of excellent display and ambi-

La Conversation is warm, cheerful, and sunny, without being kitschy.

ence. On a street that divides West Hollywood from Beverly Hills this lovely neighborhood establishment is frequented by just about everyone for miles around. Seventeen years old, La Conversation is a 1,200-square-foot space composed of a small bakery section—no larger than a very large closet—a dozen or so café tables and chairs, and a counter with five stools. Michael Carmona and Steve Carson, the owners, came to California from Philadelphia with the idea of opening a retail bakery. Steve was the baker, Michael, the manager—as befits his colorful personality. Michael's duties are at the front of the house and Steve manages the kitchen.

They started with baked goods only. Within five years they opened the café for breakfast and lunch and a year later added outdoor dining. They were quite frustrated because reviewers would not come to the delightful café or taste the goodies that Steve turned out, even though customers swore La Conversation was one of the best bakeries in Los Angeles. When a reviewer finally did arrive on the scene, La Conversation was already the "in" place, serving breakfast and lunch all day. He found that the bakery/café not only had an unusual customer base but that celebrities had already "discovered" the café.

In the early morning the entertainment crowd—producers, directors, writers, actors, and actresses—convenes. When they leave, the mid-to-late-morning crowd of neighborhood housewives and their friends takes over. The "Ladies Who Lunch" consists of visiting socialites from the East Coast who meet up with the California "Lunch Bunch." Then follows the midafternoon crowd of assorted coffee folk, plus the four-o'clock-onward "Tea and Crumpets" group, consisting of nannies, mothers, and children. And, finally, the dinner customers arrive.

Words like *cozy* and *charming* come to mind when you walk into the bakery and café. Warm, cheerful, and sunny, it looks like a feminine tearoom, or more aptly, a decorator's (which Michael is) breakfast room in a private home. It also has an outdoor terrace with several tables and chairs for guests. One would almost expect a personal invitation for breakfast, lunch, or dinner. Adding an incredible warmth to the tearoom is a wall of small framed mirrors over the antique wood counter. Other walls are hung with oil paintings as well as red-and-white and blue-and-white antique plates on beautiful wavy red-and-cream wallpaper. On the wall opposite the two utilitarian cases of baked goods (regrettably substituted for the original antique wood ones) is a collection of miniatures: wooden chairs and china tea-service items. It is charming without being kitschy. Floral displays also contributed to the beautiful interior: The fireplace mantle holds a huge and exquisite vase of tall fresh flowers, as does a corner of the mahogany counter. A small potted plant resides on each table.

Outside, awnings with burgundy, green, and yellow stripes

hang over the display windows, and red umbrellas are perched over the white café tables and chairs. A red, white, and blue sign with the store's very fetching logo announces the shop.

The bakery's patrons consist of regulars and drop-ins. As for the bakery's goodies, Michael told me that they offer 26 different kinds of desserts and pastries as well as 11 specialties of international recipes. The "High Tea" selection of three offerings consists of six assorted tea sandwiches, assorted miniscones, sweets, and a piece of celebration cake along with a variety of teas, coffee, or cappuccino, for $22 per person. La Conversation offers the whole menu in its catering operation, along with a selection of six hot and seven cold hors d'oeuvres.

On the subject of staff, the owners have a unique situation. Before they opened La Conversation they had started a successful (now closed) bakery in a location far from their current one, at which they employed two members of the same family: Graciela Cruz and her daughter Nubia. When Steve and Michael moved to the new location, the two moved with them. In the years to follow, a good part of the Cruz family joined them: Nubia's sister, cousins, brothers, and sisters-in-law. There are now three generations of Cruzes who have worked in the bakery and café. Graciela has retired and Nubia is now the daytime manager, the plum position. Nubia, now a mature woman, told me that each Cruz starts as a pot scrubber then advances to dishwasher and progresses through the ranks of kitchen helper, bus person, waiter, assistant baker, cook, sous chef, and finally to chef on different shifts according to rank and seniority.

In such an affluent and artistic location, Michael has met and become friends with many interesting people. He shared some unusual incidents with me:

Every day, without fail, a very young Beverly Hills billionaire came into the café to sit down with his $2 cup of coffee. I would chat with him whenever I could because the young man was interesting and a very nice person, and I enjoyed him. After he left, whoever the waiter was that day would find a $100 bill left on the table as a tip! One day I was admiring the billionaire's new Bentley, and he promptly replied, "It's yours, keep it. I have lots of others and someone can come pick me up here." I hastily told him I didn't want it, I was just admiring the car. But he kept insisting I take it. You know, we almost got into an argument because I wouldn't accept it!

Another customer, a lonely Parisian girl, found a home at La Conversation.

Every morning, she came in for her croissant-and-coffee breakfast. One day, she started talking to an American man sitting at the next table who happened to be a Francophile. After that, he came in every day when she was there. They were married a year later. They went to live in France, but about every six months they come back to visit and always stop in to see me. A few years ago, they came in with a baby and on the last visit with two children.

Another incident involved a very famous actress who came in for lunch.

She sat outside because she had her dog with her, and she tied the dog's leash to the table. The dog saw a bird and wanted to chase after it down busy Doheny Drive, dragging the table with him. Things went flying! The dog soon panicked, more from the weight and noise of the table than from the noise of the traffic. So the actress and I took off after the dog, which somehow had gotten injured. I insisted on taking her and the dog to my vet nearby, where the dog was stitched up. The actress couldn't thank me enough, but I felt bad because it happened on our premises. The next day she sent a humongous fresh flower arrangement by way of thanks. It took two people to carry it in.

* * *

Buosi, in Venice, Italy, is simply dazzling with its displays that are nothing short of extraordinary; it is by far the most outstanding men's shop I have seen in any of the countries in which I conducted interviews. Buosi is situated in an area 250 meters from San Marco Square, very near the Rialto Bridge. In other words, its location is smack in the middle of the tourist area, and the shopping thoroughfare in which it is located is teeming with potential customers.

Buosi opened in 1897, although owner Riccardo Bonometto has owned the shop in this particular location for more than 30 years. It is 250 square meters on two floors.

The array and display of merchandise is astonishing. Shirts, sweaters, and ties are in every color and every shade of the color spectrum. The abundance of merchandise is almost unbelievable, especially in such a small space. Jackets, coats, suits, shoes, scarves and belts, featuring the classic and the fashionable—and a mix of fabrics such as cashmere, wool, cotton, linen, leather, together with the manufactured and the bespoke—creates an ambience of "aliveness," almost a "living" entity. Never before had I encountered this feeling in a men's shop. The interior displays helped create such an ambience. Seven or so vignettes of several individual items of an outfit were grouped together, but each hung separately high up on walls, or at eye level, or wherever space was available. These showcased a *look*, a *picture*. And it was the *way* the merchandise was hung, to portray live movement, that gave such an alive quality to the shop itself.

"Everything is made in Italy with the exception of scarves, which are imported from England," one of two extremely personable and knowledgeable salesmen told me.

As for Buosi's customer base, 30 percent are Venetians and 70 percent are tourists, but of that 70 percent many are Europeans who, when they are in Italy, return to the shop for new items or wardrobes. While the manager was busy, a couple speaking in a language I couldn't understand was about to walk out with so many boxes and bags, they could barely manage.

Riccardo Bonometto told me that he does not advertise or do promotions or events because of the nature of his business. Word-of-mouth is the best advertising there is. But he holds one clearance sale a year for six weeks in the winter.

Here are some of his secrets of success:

➤ ***Location*** is the most important factor of all. If your location is bad, you can't sell the best merchandise there is.

➤ ***Personalities of salespeople*** must reflect the owner's values and philosophy, and the salespeople must like selling.

➤ ***Know your clientele.*** There must be personal rapport with your customers and you must be curious to find out about them.

➤ **_Sell quality merchandise._** The price range of your merchandise doesn't matter. What is important is that you have the highest quality possible for the price.

Prices at Buosi are reasonable, I thought, especially because the merchandise is so beautifully made.

One of Riccardo's most interesting incidents is an example of never judging customers too quickly.

Some years ago a man entered the shop and placed seven or eight million liras (about $4,000) of merchandise on the counter. He wanted to pay with a two _billion_ lira check ($220 million). I became suspicious—the check was all crumpled up—and told this man that we would go together to the bank to cash his check. The bank wouldn't cash his check. In fact everyone in the bank was laughing hilariously; every teller in the bank thought he was crazy. I thought he was crazy.

A few days later I saw a photograph in the newspaper of a man standing next to President Pertini, who was president of Italy at the time, at Geneva airport. It was the same "crazy" man who had been in the shop! I couldn't believe it. In a close-up photo he was wearing a Navy officer's jacket with many war decorations and ribbons pinned to his jacket. I don't remember now who he was or why he was with the president because what caught my eye was that next to one war decoration was attached . . . a Coca-Cola cap!

*   *   *

Jan de Luz is completely French, from the owner to the fabrics—even though it is in Carmel, California. It is a specialty niche shop with two unique features. One is a machine in the front of the shop that embroiders motifs or initials on household linens woven from natural fibers such as linen and cotton. The other is an old loom that creates this cloth of incomparable quality, situated just inside this beautiful, upscale shop.

Brigitte Luplus, along with her husband Jan, who also owns a furniture establishment a few miles from the center of Carmel, are the owners. Brigitte is the enthusiastic dynamo whose stamp is on everything she carries in the linen shop, which is actually two shops in one. Four years after opening the linen shop, Brigitte and Jan, who were so successful in their original 1,400-square-foot shop, adjoined the 1,600 square feet of space next door when it became available. The second shop became a showplace of pieces from Jan's operation: limestone mantles, tables, chairs, a wishing well, a French counter with unusual details, and a chocolatier complete with chocolate molds, among many other items. Along with these were a few different place settings of pottery dinnerware made in France.

According to Brigitte, the adjoined shops "are basically for people who have everything, whether they are locals who are all repeat customers, or tourists from all over the world who holiday in this affluent area." Her greatest innovation is the embroidery machine that, on the spot, can produce myriad patterns created on the computer connected to the embroidery machine. There are fifty different colors and an incredible array of lush thread shades.

Brigitte says people will come in asking if she can put a golf ball and a club on a dishtowel or other material, such as placemats or napkins. Or they might want a car or pet embroidered on a gift item. "Sometimes the requests are very specific," explained Brigitte,

43

"and people ask for three cats, one brown and white with greenish eyes, one gray with yellowish eyes, one black with a color of eyes in between those two others!" What Brigitte embroiders will, of course, make the customer's gift absolutely unique.

To operate the machines takes three months of training, so Brigitte and two salespeople have learned how to run it. Each must constantly take turns operating it in order not to lose the knack. Brigitte confessed that the whole process is a pain in the neck but she does it as an advertising and promotional tool—her only forms of both. She relies solely on word-of-mouth advertising because she does not believe in ads.

Brigitte's priority for her mix of merchandise is that she must like each item and that it must be exclusive. Her window displays have no specific timetable for change—they are changed as soon as the items in the window sell, which is approximately every two months. They use QuickBooks software to keep track of everything, including taxes. One of the shop's services is gift wrapping and gift boxes.

She has learned from experience to listen closely to her customers.

> When we first came here from France, I brought almost everything wrong for American tastes—the colors of the cotton and linen fabrics, the size of the soaps were too big, as were other items. So I listened to my customers or I would be out of business. For instance, since I design my own fabrics I changed tablecloths, which nobody uses here, to placemats.

One customer, a tourist, said, "If I could, I would take half of this shop home with me." Another customer told me, "I bring friends and family and employees here from my floral shop in Peoria, Illinois, where I have several businesses. The men love the oversized French antiques and the limestone pieces, and the women love the soaps that the owner designs, the robes, and the dishtowels." This customer was particularly pleased that the linens were hand cut and hand sewn in the shop, and that they can each have their own patterns embroidered and monograms added.

One incredible experience that gave Brigitte insight into customer service occurred some years ago. A customer who bought many items asked the price of an antique French candy jar displayed in the window. Brigitte explained that it was not for sale because it was rare. Actually, Brigitte and her husband loved the piece and had planned to use it in a house they were furnishing. The customer insisted and said, "Don't be silly, we are in the United States, everything has a price. How much is it?" Not knowing what to do and not wanting to offend the customer, Brigitte called her husband who also did not want to sell the piece. He told her to say the price was $5,000, thinking the woman would never pay that much because it was probably closer to $1,000 in value. "She bought it," Brigitte said with amazement.

* * *

Papier Mâché is an extraordinary niche shop in Venice, Italy, and one of the greatest examples of handmade manufacture and retail combinations I have come across. What could be a more outstanding business to find than a mask shop? I asked myself as I roamed around Venice. As tea is to England and women's couture to Paris, masks are to Venice.

Fascinated by the extraordinary workmanship of the masks in the display window, I entered a bright, cheerful space where, in one area, a man's hands were plunged into what appeared to be dough. Immediately he arose, wiped off his hands, and with a big smile introduced himself to me as Stefano Gottardo, the owner. He opened the shop in 1977 as a project to re-establish the tradition of mask making, because that was the year in which the centuries-old tradition of Carnivale was reintroduced after a long lapse. When he realized that masks were an absolutely essential part of Carnivale costumes, and determined to perfect the art of papier maché masks in which he had a long-standing interest, he "revolutionized" the process with his new ideas and use of new materials. Self-taught, Stefano calls himself a perfectionist who loves his work and says his ambition has always been to achieve the highest quality of workmanship possible.

Masks are created for opera and theater companies, Venice's Carnivale, and party-givers and –goers from round the world.

Stefano is the maker of the molds; his wife, Eliana, is the principal painter. Seated at her own workstation in full view of potential customers on the other side of the picture window, Senora Gottardo explained to me that she is an artist who (along with three others in the busier season) takes about 20 hours to complete a mask. Eliana often copies from paintings of famous figures and characters in opera, theatre, and cinema. She also replicates the colors from the museum paintings found in the art books from which Stefano has designed and made the molds. Manuela, Stefano's sister, is the chief salesperson and completes the Gottardo triumvirate.

This is a niche business like no other. To tour Papier Mâché is to experience a fantasy kingdom. As we walked around the shop, I marveled at the large, small, odd-shaped, spectacular, amusing, or just plain pretty masks of every hue and kind that lined the shelves and walls. We came upon Gottardo's collection of white, lifelike figures from the Commedia dell'Arte that he sculpted from clay, which were astonishingly original and realistic.

Besides being a mold maker and sculptor, Stefano is a teacher. He employs apprentices, one or more at a time, "who must come from one of the Venetian art schools; then they must serve a three-year apprenticeship" of mold making and designing. He encourages them to learn everything possible, but most of all to contribute new ideas, which he adopts if possible.

About 20 percent of the customers are opera and theatre companies as well as party givers and partygoers from around the world, so of course Papier Mâché ships worldwide. The other 80 percent of the business comes from the tourist trade. About one percent is bought for home décor, either by interior designers or individuals.

Stefano's timetable for making masks begins in September, when the Gottardos start discussing ideas and making final decisions; in October he starts the molds and finishes them by November; in December they begin the painting, which is completed about the end of February or beginning of March. In the meantime, ribbons and ornaments of all kinds—which come in all colors—are selected to attach to the masks that will actually match costumes. Large masks are worn at the Carnivale parade; small ones are preferred for the many private parties.

The price of a mask starts at approximately $30 for small ones and goes as high as $350 for large ones. When queried about the secrets of his success, Stefano offered just two. First, he says, be *friends* with each other (personnel) and with customers, and know how to speak to customers. Second, he educates children about mask making so they will have an appreciation of the artistic mode. "Children are the customers of the future," says Stefano.

Papier Mâché has had many write-ups in guidebooks, magazines, tourist publications, and newspapers, which Stefano says are the best form of advertising. He does not believe in formal advertising per se. Word-of-mouth has brought some interesting customers to his shop, including the vice president of Russia, who had seen a Papier Mâché mask at a ball. He arrived at the shop with two bodyguards, looked around, engaged in friendly, quiet conversation with Stefano, told a few jokes, laughed a lot, and bought two large, beautiful, expensive masks for gifts.

Chapter 3

Location, Location, Location

Location, location, location is almost a mantra in the retail field—it is that important.

If the type of shop you're thinking about already exists where you want to establish your business, you will create an overload by opening another. If your town or city has too many linen establishments, or candle shops, or whatever you plan to sell, you would be foolish to open a similar shop unless you've spotted a market for something completely new and different that no other retailer carries. That's asking for trouble.

If, however, you've determined that your niche shop will be unique in the area, then you can tentatively plan your location. But you'll need to do further research before you make your final decision, and you need to work backward for a moment and think about who your customers will be before deciding where your shop will be. Who are you appealing to, both generally and specifically? All males, both men and boys? Or just younger men between the ages of 18 and 40? Is age going to be a factor? Does your shop appeal to new parents, senior citizens, people who knit, or local or foreign tourists? What economic bracket are you aiming for: upscale income, student budgets, or middle-class two-income families?

Demographics

After deciding what type of customers your niche will appeal to, you need to know if the local residents or tourists will fit that customer criteria. The statistical characteristics of the potential customers in your area are called *demographics*, and they usually include the median income of an area's residents, a breakdown of how people are employed, average prices of homes and rentals, tourism statistics, and other good information from which to get a general idea of potential customers. So it's important to know your potential customer base. If, for example, you know that your niche products will appeal to college-age students, but you live in an area where there is no college or even a high school, your chances of finding customers to sustain your business are very slim. If your niche will be high-end but demographics show a low median income for your area, again your shop stands a poor chance of being successful. Your location must take into account the demographics of the area in relation to your niche product.

You can research the demographics for your prospective location on the Internet, at the local chamber of commerce, at city hall, and simply by asking established owners in the location you are considering. Of course, some might not want to help you, particularly if your shop would compete in any way with theirs, so it would be unproductive to approach them. But if you choose shops that are not selling anything remotely close to what you are planning to sell, you will find some owners willing to give you first-hand information about the customer base of the local area. It's also a good idea to travel to niche shops that would be similar to yours but are in another city or state—far enough away that you would not be competing—to check out their inventory, ask the owners why they chose their locations, and get information about their customer base.

In addition to demographics, you need to consider longevity factors of the location. Will that adjacent parking lot remain a parking lot, or are plans in the works to demolish it and build condos, thereby leaving your shop with no convenient customer parking? Is the street well lit at night so that customers will shop after dark? (It's a good idea to visit an area after dark to see if there are any negative elements to the neighborhood.) Are there cafés or restaurants nearby where customers can stop for lunch before or after browsing your shop? Are there established hotels, motels, businesses, or a post office nearby to create foot traffic past your business? Are there established tourist attractions nearby so that you can promote your shop in tourism brochures or tourism Internet sites? Is your location easily accessed by cars, buses, subways? Are there sidewalks or walkways for pedestrians?

As for the parking situation, you must decide how important attached parking is to your type of business or whether nearby street parking is adequate enough. Or whether both would serve you even better. If your business plan includes selling 70 percent of your merchandise on the Internet, then foot traffic is slightly less important to you than it would be if you didn't have a website. If you plan to open an apparel business, it may be to your advantage to be located in the center of a downtown area or at the crossroads of two busy streets. You may need to depend on foot traffic and, of course, parking would be a consideration. All these factors must be taken into account when choosing a location.

What Not to Look For

Recognizing undesirable locations is equally important but not always as simple as it seems. Over the years countless shops have opened in shopping centers featuring huge national discount chains, and the owners have assumed that customers from these chain stores would overflow into their little shops. And the leases were probably affordable! But they surely forgot to take into account that these shopping centers are often in barren areas on the edge of town, forlorn and ill-lit. If they had visited these centers after dark, they might have noticed that, in general, the customers of the discount warehouses would park, shop at the warehouse, then leave the area. There was nothing inviting or attractive enough about the surroundings that would make them want to wander to other small shops after dark.

An example of a recent closing I witnessed was a lovely-in-every-way apparel shop, isolated from other similar business establishments by a bicycle shop, two nondescript stores, and two cafeteria-style eateries. It was located at the wrong end of a small city and just couldn't sustain enough foot traffic. Don't decide on a location solely on the basis of a "good" or a "great" lease deal with good parking!

Carmel, California

Seeing the demographics of a popular tourist area will give you a fuller picture of the related retail categories.

For example, the principal industry of Carmel—part of Monterey County, California—is shops (all 328 of them)* and a few stores. Most exist in the one square mile of Carmel-by-the-Sea that has a

*Statistics accurate as of March 20, 2005.

permanent population of 4,100 residents. Carmel is a paradise of oceanside beauty, with its charming homes, courtyards, gardens, and, of course, shops, which make it one of the best-known tourist centers in the U.S. To accommodate the thousands of visitors yearly, Carmel boasts 42 hotels, inns, and bed-and-breakfasts. The allure of the town is not hurt by the presence of former mayor Clint Eastwood, now a businessman in addition to his other profession of actor and director, who is unequivocally respected as a concerned citizen.

Carmel shop owners are right in line with the general tendency today to open more than one shop of the same type after success with the first. One successful Carmel interior designer who owned a home furnishings operation that consisted primarily of furniture opened a second shop, again with furniture and giftware, but with an emphasis on lighting. Now there is a third shop featuring all of the above plus table linens and bed linens. Each shop is about the same size but the merchandise carried is determined by the *location*—a very important point.

In my experience, what is true of shops in Carmel is true of shops everywhere. The more successful the owners become, the greater the need or desire to expand. Usually they start in a less desirable location and expand for reasons of space, location, or to add an additional category—or for all three reasons. They work toward obtaining the most affluent or appropriate location possible.

Remarkably, Carmel boasts 80 art galleries, 42 women's apparel shops, and 22 home furnishings shops. The categories of its 328 retail establishments—only a few are stores—break down as follows:

Category	*Total*
Accessories—Men & Women	10
Antiques	17
Apparel—Children	7

Apparel—Men	3
Apparel—Women	42
Apparel—Men & Women	9
Arts & Crafts	4
Bakeries*	2
Beauty Care**	8
Bookshops	3
Drugs	1
Fabrics, Sewing, Yarns	4
Florists, Garden	6
Galleries: Paintings, Photography, Framing, Others, and Combinations	80
Gifts & Accessories	15
Groceries, Food, Cheese, Candy***	10
Hardware	1
Home Furnishings, Lighting	22
—Kitchenware	5
—Linens	4
—Cutlery	2
Jewelry, Gems	34
Miscellaneous	6
Music	3
Optical	2
Pet Supplies, Animals	3
Pipes, Tobacco, Spirits	4
Resale	4
Shoes	8
Stationery, Cards, Pens	6
Toys	2
Travel	1

*Not included are food shops with seating of any kind; no cafés or restaurants.
** Not included are service shops such as beauty salons.
*** No supermarkets or chains.

The 80 art galleries represent Carmel's reputation, begun in the 1920s, as a haven for artists and art lovers. Other tourist spots around the world have their own special retail emphasis. In Windsor, England—home to Windsor Castle—for example, some shops do a fine mini-niche business in royal souvenir items. Many shops near SeaWorld in San Diego, California, offer marine-related mementos as a mini-niche category. And in Geneva, Switzerland, a popular mini-niche category is Swiss watches. If you plan to carry items that reflect a special retail emphasis in your area, your inventory should be different from other shops. Each of the 80 art galleries in Carmel, for example, offer different categories of art and artists, so they are not competing with the same merchandise.

The right location is of prime importance as compared with just the good location. Never settle for a less-than-ideal location just because the rent is cheap and you think you can somehow work around the problems!

* * *

The free advice from the successful owners who were interviewed for this book can help you understand the importance of location from the very beginning. In the following success stories, notice the location of each shop in the upcoming examples and certain factors emerge and re-emerge. For instance, several shop owners rented premises near a hotel, inn, motel, or other hostelries for tourists or businesspeople because they determined that these people would fit the customer criteria for their merchandise. As a potential shop owner, these stories will also give you an inside look at the stock, customer service, longevity factors, and ambience that makes these shops so successful.

▶ Success Stories

To survive in a large city, in an area that more often than not houses national chain stores, it is necessary to be outstanding and to offer customers merchandise they are simply not going to find anywhere else. ***Helia's*** is one such shop, located in Georgetown, Washington, D.C., where the population includes affluent professionals, government employees, and businesspeople; students from the various colleges in the area; and tourists.

More than two-thirds of the main shopping area in Georgetown (Wisconsin Avenue at M Street, a busy thoroughfare) is composed of chain stores and hip shops for college students and various ethnic groups. Less than a quarter is composed of shops catering to

Helia's location enjoys lots of foot traffic and nearby parking, and just a few doors away is the best-known hotel, the Georgetown Inn.

the local businesspeople, professionals, government employees, and better-heeled tourists.

It was at that busy juncture that I found charming Helia's, which was located near a parking lot, on-street parking, a bus stop, and a subway stop. After looking around for only a few minutes, I was approached by a saleswoman who commented about the unusual earrings I was wearing. As she was talking, she unobtrusively walked over to a display, slipped off an equally unusual necklace that coordinated beautifully with the earrings, and brought it over for me to see. Subtly, she had introduced an item that I might not have seen, and she made me aware of the knock-out drama of the combination. Unfortunately, I couldn't squeeze the necklace into my budget that day, but already I regret not buying it.

Mariam Heydari started Helia's 20 years ago. Both owner and designer, she found that outfits of two, three, and four layers of free-flowing, easy, artsy clothes were just what women in government and those in the "upper class and business" wanted to wear for both daytime and evening—ensembles that were different, unusual, and easy to pack for traveling.

Today Mariam is joined in her business by Omid Zajiakhami, her son, who designs unique fabrics in sophisticated colors. They collaborate to add the finishing touches. She designs 50 to 60 outfits every three months, inspired by the fashions of the 1800s and 1920s and by the colors of the 1960s. Because Mariam designs each garment herself, her inventory control system is all in her head.

One regular customer raved about Mariam, who, she said, listens to her customers and is very personable. In addition to viewing the seasonal collections, this customer looks forward to chatting with her. Another local customer told me that Mariam creates a unique product. "It doesn't exist anywhere else. So having bought one outfit, one will always come back for another." And the complaint of an international tourist is, "Why can't I find you else-where? Your shop is so unique. It's not the same as you see all over the world."

Mariam chose her location because there is lots of foot traffic, parking nearby, and, importantly, the best-known hotel, the Georgetown Inn, is just a few doors away. Because the shop is sur-rounded by funky stores and chain stores, Helia's stands out imme-diately, as does a new upscale children's shop a few doors away. The shop has a placard out front that proclaims it sells organic clothing—a terrific gimmick that seems appropriate for the area.

Like many of the successfully established shop owners I inter-viewed, Mariam does no advertising. Her business is all word-of-mouth. She describes her shop's ambience as "European. Intimate and personal. For instance, not using mannequins is more per-sonal."

The combination of fairly small crystal chandeliers, simple re-cessed lighting, and bare frosted light bulbs creates an eclectic and startlingly dramatic effect. Mariam told me that for the first few years she used all chandeliers but soon realized that they didn't do justice to the inventory because the shop is naturally dark.

Her secret of success is good service, quality merchandise, and inventory in abundance. "When you put on a garment you have to love it immediately. If you have to think about it, don't buy it. If you immediately feel it needs a scarf, a pin, a *something,* don't buy it." Mariam is completely honest with her customers, and that's a very important part of good service.

Being in Washington, Mariam has seen her share of an eclectic mix of customers, but none so startling as on one Sunday morning in 1983, the day before the grand opening of the store.

We were still working inside the shop, nailing and tacking, although the window displays were done, when a really scruffy, disheveled-looking man with wild hair, unshaven, and wearing torn blue jeans, walked in, pointed to an ensemble in the window and said, "I'll take that. I need size 8 and that looks like it." He didn't even ask the price! It was about $900, I think. Anyway, I was new to the business and nervous, and this was the first customer. I told him it wasn't size 8 and went to look for one. Meanwhile I was thinking that the man didn't look like he could afford anything, and how was I going to handle this? As it turned out, he had been right and the outfit in the window was size 8. I asked him if he had a credit card which, to my relief, he produced, and told me that he knew his wife would really like the outfit. I asked him for his address. He said, "Here or in London?" London? So I said both, which he gave me. By this time I was really mystified. Then I asked for his phone number. Again he said, "Here or in London?" Again I took both, and he told me to send the package to his London address because his wife was there, and he was doing a concert here. A concert? I looked at his name and certainly had never heard of him. So when I got home that night I asked my son, "Did you ever hear of a Mick Jagger?"

* * *

Candlesticks of Carmel, owned by sisters Susie Shirokow and Leslie Bruhn, began at just 300 square feet. In 2004 they added another 200 square feet of selling space by opening up a back room. Originally, the size and location of the shop caused some trepidation for Shirokow and Bruhn. Although the shop is on the corner of a main shopping street, it is situated below street level, beneath another business, and five steps down! In fact, the location turned out to be "excellent, couldn't be better," according to Susie. "Customers feel like they've found a secret shop." One of their most important advertising sources turned out to be their niche product itself, and it happened by accident: the gorgeous scents from all the candles wafts up to the sidewalk and draws the tourists down the steps to their shop.

In addition to candles and candlesticks, their merchandise has grown to include home accessories, so it is now in the category of a gift shop. Of candles alone, they stock about 20 categories and styles. "We are constantly searching for the new and innovative." says Susie. Tourists are 75 percent of their business; locals, 25 percent. One of their best promotions is taking a percentage off for "special event" weekends (when hundreds of tourists are in town) and offering incentives such as "buy three and get one free." Providing great personal service and a natural stick-to-it attitude through bad times as well as good are part of their successful assets. Here is some of the sisters' advice to new businesses:

➤ Be sure to have enough financial backing to pay bills and buy enough merchandise for two years.

➤ As soon as you have a hot-selling item, reorder quickly. As soon as you notice a cold item, put it on sale and promote it quickly within the shop. Susie also calls this "PM," which stands for "push money." Part of the profit goes to the staff member who sold the item.

* * *

Who would ever dream that selling pens would provide a living, let alone become a highly successful business? Detlef Bittner dreamed the dream, and by adding appropriate accoutrements, his shop is an outstanding example of creating a niche business from what you love.

Bittner—The Pleasure of Writing, also in Carmel, California, is a shop of fine writing instruments—high-quality pens and limited editions of collectors' pens. Customers can also find beautiful accoutrements, such as a display of colored inks in a showcase, pen chests, catalogs of custom stationery, invitations, announcements, and leather journals. The elegant shop, located on a main thoroughfare of Carmel, is constructed of stone, glass, and wood, and the 400-square-foot interior was designed by the owners. Detlef Bittner came by his love of the finest writing materials in Europe, where he grew up. Together with his wife, Cynthia, he originally opened his business in a courtyard that contained a few other small businesses but was tucked away from the main stream of tourists. After eight years there, they relocated to their current location in 2000, which has proved to be an excellent decision. The clients of this specialty shop are writers, business executives, and collectors. About 25 percent of the customers are locals, 65 percent are from the rest of the United States (including some tourists), and 10 percent are international. The customers in the last two categories find Bittner through its website (www.bittner.com) and from advertising in specialty magazines.

* * *

Cottage of Sweets is a doll-size cottage in Carmel, California. A little more than 200 square feet, it is filled with over 600 different kinds of candies. Lanny and Linda Rose bought this British sweet shop in 1980, and Lanny says the cottage is the manifestation of the candy store in the *Harry Potter* books. In addition to a full line of British goodies, there are 50 different varieties of licorice imported from all over the world and a full line of chocolates—

from crèmes to caramels, truffles to toffees, and nut clusters in milk and dark chocolate that are made in a nearby chocolate factory. Until they sold it a few years ago, Lanny and two partners owned the factory.

On Thursdays during the winter months, Lanny makes the fudge. During the summer tourist season this increases to three days a week. Linda arranges all the edible products in display cases and on shelves and handles the flower arrangements. She also gardens the small plot in front of the shop.

A candy shop is all about appearances, sparkling and fresh.

Cottage of Sweets is located on the main street of Carmel because, Lanny explained, foot traffic is imperative for a candy shop. Seven others closed in the last few years because of poor locations, unimaginative interiors, or uninviting exteriors—all unacceptable in Lanny's book. "A candy shop is all about appearance: sparkling, fresh, and colorful. A customer will buy something the first time because of this but come back because the candy tasted good." Eighty percent of the customer base is tourists and 20 percent is local. "Family businesses do well in hard economic times, but sweet shops do exceptionally well in bad times because everyone can afford a few pieces of candy when they can't afford bigger ticket items for the kids," explained Lanny.

They advertise on a colorful local map that reaches almost all tourists, plus they purchase ads in programs at the local repertory

Cottage of Sweets' location allows it to take advantage of pedestrian traffic.

theatre. As a special promotion he gives two-pound boxes of chocolates, a $35 donation, to silent auctions for any charity that needs his help. Lanny and Linda attend two gourmet food and gift shows each year, where they do their buying.

Here is their most important advice to potential niche shop owners:

➤ The Internet is opening up new avenues of purchasing/selling.

➤ Know your product line.

➤ Do your homework.

➤ Know why things are working or why they're not.

* * *

Nature's Bounty by the Sea, in Carmel, California, is a wonderful example of a single-category, niche shop. Every gem and mineral in stock (including crystals, jade, amber, coral, and fossils), its bronze display pieces, and its carvings evolved from nature. Spectacular displays in dramatically lit, tall wood cabinets and on tables highlight the merchandise to its greatest advantage. Rick Nunez, who owns Nature's Bounty with his partner, Dan Barthel, have been in what they call their "dream shop" for 10 years, after being in an obscure location for seven years. Their 850-square-foot shop is in a tourist area providing all the foot traffic they could desire.

Word-of-mouth has been sufficient advertising in the past for this established business with repeat customers. However, online sales now account for about 10 percent of the shop's international clientele, and this is growing. Tourists from around the United States comprise about 30 percent of the shop's customers, and 60 percent are local. Here is Rick and Dan's advice:

➤ You must love people.

➤ Superb customer service is imperative.

➤ Be as knowledgeable as possible about your merchandise and pass on as much of your knowledge to your customers as you can.

➤ Courtesy is absolutely essential.

➤ The customer is always right.

As you can see, a good location does not always mean owning the largest shop in the most expensive shopping area of town. It entails using demographics to match your shop with your potential customers.

Chapter 4

Creating Mini-Boutiques

If your location and customer demographics show that more than one type of niche category could be popular in your shop, consider the concept of mini-boutiques—areas within your shop that are set aside and displayed individually for each niche category.

Several shopowners that I interviewed have discovered that their locations can support good sales in different niche categories and have created a mini-boutique for each niche, creating niche-shops-within-a-shop. They have been remarkably successful with this concept. Three that stand out are Landis, Why Not, and KRML.

* * *

Landis General Store sounds like it should be located in a small town on the East Coast or in the Midwest. Actually, it's located on *the* shopping street of Larchmont Village at the edge of what was once one of the chicest residential sections of Los Angeles: Hancock Park.

Landis General Store contains many mini-shops, or mini-boutiques, within its 3,200 square feet. The shop is composed of three different 900-square-foot sections of selling space, a 450-square-foot rear section, and extra space taken up by connectors and other factors. But it did not start out with so much space. It began small, and during their 14 years in business the owners acquired additional space by annexing two adjacent shops that went out of business. Openings through the connecting walls enlarged the original shop into one cohesive whole that exudes the air of intimacy and ambience of a genuine country general store.

Its original name was Landis Department Store, owned by a Mr. Landis, and it was located directly across the street from its present location. But when Landis closed his store in 1990, customers were "hysterical," according to the present owners, Chris Wolfus and Edie Frère, who were acquaintances of Landis's. "Why not open a miniature department store?" Landis asked Edie and Chris, for he knew their background. Together they had run charity boutiques as well as a catalog business out of their homes. Chris has a business degree and now does the accounting. Edie had spent 10 years with the U.S. Department of State, in the Protocol office and at embassies abroad.

Landis mentored them in business practices for a year (and worked for them as well), and they already had their own firm beliefs about retailing, as well as realistic goals.

For instance, Chris and Edie knew they wanted to stock as much inventory as possible with the start-up funds available to them; this was more important to them than spending their limited funds on an expensive décor. Indeed, in the area of finances, Landis stands out as one of the finest examples of the shops represented here.

They both agreed they wanted "a country-store feel," which was the essence of Landis's original store. Another of their goals was "to fit into the neighborhood." By the looks of the shop today, they certainly have achieved that goal. On a practical basis they chose a country look because it was cheaper to create—they could buy secondhand items and inexpensive materials, such as Lodgepole pine boards for molding and floor tiles by the case at a local source in Los Angeles. By picking everything themselves, they got exactly what they wanted. Because Edie had to lug all of it back to the shop in her station wagon, every purchase needed to fit in her car. They then found an inexpensive treasure of a carpenter who "did everything."

The partners' original buying plan was divided into two categories: merchandise and décor. They knew how much they had to spend and how to divide it. So their budget was based on a three-year plan further divided into three parts: merchandise, décor, and a "fall back" fund. The latter is one element of their success, along with an abiding belief in only taking moderate markups. Their budget is based on a two- to three-year plan depending upon circumstances.

On the subject of their customers, Chris and Edie say that 60 to 65 percent are not from the Hancock Park neighborhood, because Larchmont Village has become, to some degree, a Los Angeles historical site and, as such, people travel from all over the city and environs to look and shop.

In sharing their innovations and secrets, Edie and Chris explained that the mini-boutiques evolved into the ten they have today:

1. Notions (for example, ribbons by the yard—"Nobody carries them anymore," the owners said.)
2. Toys and baby.
3. Women's accessories—hats and purses.
4. Jewelry.
5. Gifts—frames, table linens, kitchen accessories, tabletop (individual china pieces, lamps).
6. Business and art supplies, scrapbooks (a result of customer requests).
7. Paper goods and wrapping paper.
8. Greetings cards.
9. Stationery—includes stationery supplies and custom invitations (and grew out of customer requests).
10. Books—cookbooks, specialty, and boutique gift books (and one book that is a niche in itself, according to Edie, entitled *Tiffany's Table Manners for Teenagers*).

Chris and Edie's buying philosophy is based on category of need—no matter what it is—which is how and why they expand. They are not concerned if a new category has no relationship to the rest of the shop's merchandise. Their business philosophy also includes the following:

➤ They do not buy fads, but they do buy fun items (such as a golf-cart rocking horse for children), which constitute an area of need as well as another niche.

➤ Their buying reflects their customers' tastes, not their own personal tastes.

➤ Timing is a secret of their buying.

➤ Customer service is a priority: even if there is only one request for an item, they will order it.

➤ They offer a personal buying service. A shut-in or a business person who cannot go to the shop to buy something for themselves or as a gift may have it selected for them from the customer's suggestion list. The item is then gift wrapped and hand-delivered or mailed to the recipient.

➤ They offer free gift wrapping and many choices of wrapping paper, which the shop stocks.

➤ Personnel is like family—several employees have worked there for many years.

Merchandise in some of the mini-boutiques turns over faster than others, but the turns on certain specific items are truly amazing. (If you are not familiar with *turns*, see Chapter 5, "Finances.") Landis General Store has a surprising number of turns per year for these items:

➤ Picture frames: 8–10

➤ Doormats: 8–10

➤ Patio furniture: approximately 8

➤ Thank-you notes: 6–8

➤ Toys: 6–8

➤ Socks, slippers: 6

➤ Small leather goods: 6

Chris and Edie don't conduct frequent sales, because they do not need to. But when they do, they start at 25 percent off and move rapidly to 40-50 percent off.

Another very important secret of success that they are willing to share is what they term their "homework," which consists of two valuable pieces of advice for start-up owners:

➤ Read everything possible for clues to new trend items or categories. If something emerges from five different reading

Thank-you note niche display at Landis General Store, Los Angeles, California.

materials, for instance, it may indicate a new trend—which usually starts on the East or West Coasts.

➤ Go to a variety of gift shows. Each will present items and ideas or even a new product line that could possibly create a niche for you or, at the least, additions to an established category of merchandise. (The partners themselves attend gifts shows in San Francisco, New York, Atlanta, Dallas, Seattle, and occasionally in England.)

Starting a new business involves dealing with all sorts of problems, humorously illustrated by a story that Edie related to me.

A few years ago, after a fumigator had come to deal with pests next door, we had an upsurge in our bug population and a migration of them through the connecting walls into a room at the back of the store. We only became aware of the problem when we heard screams coming from the room. Bugs were running wild! But our always-resourceful customers, who happened to be older ones that day, simply grabbed nearby stools, stood on them, and continued to read cards in our greeting card department. Our staff was far more distraught than our customers!

The concept of Landis General Store is exactly what a general store of the past—or present—should be: a store devoted to selling items, products, and categories. But the ambience of this particular general store is like no other. It's a collection of shops—delightful, charming, and warm in feeling—and it is a superb example of retailing's Golden Rule: the right item, in the right place, at the right time, for the right price.

*   *   *

Why Not is a children's retail operation that at 4,800 square feet cannot, in all honesty, be called a shop. It is divided into several

small boutiques, which gives it the intimate *feel* and ambience of a shop. It is a unique store in every way, located at the corner of the main street in the Old Town section of Alexandria, Virginia. Why Not resides in a lovely old brick building that was once a small factory and before that a hospital during the Civil War. Its location, states owner Kate Schlabach, is "the best corner in the best block in Old Town."

Why Not makes the most of its historic building, once a hospital during the Civil War.

Tourist buses let tourists off at the top of the block where the tourist council is located, and the people wander down the street. Almost the first thing they see are the charming window displays of Why Not. "It has become," said Kate, "a destination location, meaning that customers head down to the store because after 40 years in operation it has become an institution." And that surely is the most distinguished appellation any store can hope to achieve.

There are all kinds of gift shops, and Why Not is one of the best because not only can customers shop for their own children, but they can also find unusual, original, generally one-of-a-kind gifts, whether they're toys, apparel, or a plethora of accessories.

The mix of merchandise is one of the unique features of Why Not, with its "not to be found anywhere in the area" European clothing and toys—which represent 40 percent of the stock. The other 60 percent is devoted to special domestic lines and items.

There is a costume corner for "dress-up," another boutique of books and dolls (such as the Madeline collection), games, a garden corner and puppets, a tiny area of "different" shoes and boots, bonnets and hats, and bows and barrettes. In addition to wearing apparel, there is a small section of CDs and cards, dozens of stuffed animals of every sort, bins of children's collectibles, and a large, well-equipped play area.

Because gifts play a large part of purchases, there are at least 10 choices of gift wrapping and 15 choices of ribbons. Why Not charges a nominal fee for its gift wrapping (as opposed to many similar shops that charge outrageous prices).

The other factor that contributes to the ambience—the uniqueness of Kate Schlabach's enterprise—are the antique pieces, fitting for a library, perhaps, in such a historic city but uncommon and refreshingly innovative in a children's store. Some of the antiques are unusual in themselves or, as Kate put it, "different" in her utilization of them. Instead of a stepstool, as almost all stores would use, she utilizes a brass and wood sliding ladder from an old hardware company to reach items high up, thereby accomplishing two goals at once: a put-to-good-use antique piece became an innovation that, in turn, contributed to the interior ambience.

Likewise, the large, floor-to-ceiling wood apothecary cabinet once at home in a pharmacy but converted now into two separate parts: one half, with many small drawers, displays reproduction tin toys and old books such as the one about a rabbit that is surrounded by stuffed rabbits, and is used downstairs; the other half, upstairs, contains Playmobile toys.

When I visited this shop-within-a shop, one longtime employee described the store as a "hip" shop whose customers are young, with-it, affluent people who are helped at the store by, for the most part, older women who have already raised their own children. At Christmas time, she added, young businessmen, as well as the young women, shop at Why Not for gifts.

Kate said her greatest assets are "personnel and service." She added that some of her personnel worked at the store as kids, went out into the world, and have come back to work there. I wondered what had drawn them back, and Kate explained that the first two secrets of her success are: "You must love having *fun*," and "Have *fun* with customers."

Why Not does only one special promotional event each year. "People know us for the Scottish Walk parade that has taken place at the start of the Christmas season for more than 20 years." The tradition has been to stop at Why Not at the end of the parade to see the longtime Santa, "who's very humorous; kids and adults alike adore him."

Kate's advice to would-be shop owners echoed that of so many owners I met and observed: *love* what you do, find your *niche*, and don't try to copy someone else's success.

* * *

If **KRML** sounds like a radio station, it is! It's also a retail shop, a recording studio, a broadcast studio, and a concert venue. All 1,010 square feet is uniquely designed so that it can be converted at a moment's notice into any of these options. The front window display is actually the live broadcast studio facing a busy street where people can look in and enjoy what's going on. Once located in a small out-of-the-way shop known only to jazz lovers, KRML's retail location is today prominently located where the "world head-quarters of jazz is part of the community," in the Eastwood building (yes, as in Clint Eastwood), in Carmel, California. Owner David Kimball and his partners' connection with Eastwood goes back many years. Eastwood is a jazz aficionado and jazz composer in addition to the many other hats he wears.

KRML's 1,010 square feet is uniquely designed as a retail shop, a recording studio, a broadcast studio, and a concert venue. Photo by Jim Bourne.

Sometimes Eastwood stops in at KRML, sits at the piano, and plays jazz or his famous "Misty." Because "Clint" is a big draw, there is a popular section of the shop that sells CDs and DVDs of Clint Eastwood music and films. And it's not unusual for people to walk in asking breathlessly, "Where is Clint? I want to say hello!" or bring things in saying casually, "Can you give this to Clint for me?" or even write "Hi Clint! Remember me?" on the memo line of checks.

Kimball says KRML is the only radio station he knows of that has a retail operation. KRML sells apparel, jazz and blues CDs, videos, DVDs, musical instruments (percussion and guitar), original art (paintings and photographs), frames, posters, books, stationery, note cards, clocks, musical novelty watches, and small electronics. Everything pertains to jazz, reflecting the station's jazz niche.

Foot traffic is heavy in the area because it is located on a main street in Carmel. It is surrounded by popular restaurants, motels, a gas station, art galleries, and there is a tourist information center next door. Kimball also places ads and articles in three area newspapers, four national magazines, and in programs at several art events. In addition, KRML streams music on the Internet through its website, reaching an almost-worldwide audience.

For special promotions, KRML has created three unique "subscription" programs that offer concerts (in the shop) and receptions with well-known jazz musicians, gourmet dinners at participating restaurants, several items of wearing apparel and artist CDs, along with other goodies, all for one price depending on the subscription program chosen.

This multiuse niche shop is incredibly unique in its presentation, giving KRML an unusual cozy feel that adds to its ambience.

Chapter 5

Finances

If the financial side of business is foreign to you, the first thing you need to know is where to get help. If you took advantage of downloading and completing the business planning forms from the Service Corps of Retired Executives (SCORE) website, as I suggested in Chapter 1, you will now have a realistic overview of your expected financial outlay. Now it is essential to attend some basic business seminars, which you can find at local colleges, adult evening classes, private companies advertising on the Internet, and at SCORE, which is a resource partner with the Small Business Administration (SBA). Because SCORE seminars and consultations are free, I am including information on these as a guide to what you should look for in a well-rounded business course.

SCORE Advice*

A SCORE planning course teaches about business plans, financing, taxes, licenses, permits, bookkeeping, and start-up costs.

*Courtesy of the Monterey Bay chapter of SCORE.

To quote from one of its brochures, SCORE is an "independent non-profit association comprised of 12,400 *volunteer* counselors nationwide with 389 chapters; the counselors are retired business owners or business executives." SCORE volunteers provide professional guidance and information to small-business owners, including individual counseling and mentoring, workshops, and online counseling via e-mail. To make an appointment to discuss any aspect of either a start-up business or an ongoing one in your local area, you will find all the information you need at www.score.org.

It is that easy to get help!

Typically, three topics are discussed in a two- or three-hour symposium:

1. ***Business Financing:*** How to get a loan, what a bank wants to know about you and your business, and the need to write a business plan
2. ***Legal Matters:*** What kind of agreement you need, what your lease obligations are, how to protect your business name
3. ***Accounting:*** What type of record-keeping system you need to start up a business, how to handle tax returns, and the collection of sales taxes

A typical SCORE business workshop will cover three things:

1. ***An Expanded Version of Self-Assessment:*** What it takes to start a successful business, which may include topics of personal traits, whether the business is right for you, and whether your business can succeed.
2. ***Market Research:*** An expanded version of questions to answer in regard to your market research.

3. ***A Business Plan:*** The map leading to a profitable shop. Among other objectives, it helps with raising money. Banks require a business plan if you seek a loan from them. It's also used as a benchmark to compare actual performance of the business with the plan, and it identifies flaws and omissions in your business concept.

A business plan should include:

➤ A business description

➤ A description of the merchandise

➤ A description of your marketing and sales strategies

➤ Detailed operating requirements

➤ A detailed financial plan that answers the following questions:

What are your expected start-up costs?

How did you arrive at these numbers?

How will the money be obtained?

How long will it take to turn a profit?

How much of your capital will you use before you turn a profit?

➤ Detailed financial projections that include the following, among other factors:

Projected income and expenses for 24 months, itemized by expense category

Projected cash flow statement for the period of time until you realistically expect to turn a profit

➤ A summary and overview of the business and of the plan, including:

A short overview describing the business

A summary of your goals and objectives

A short essay of your qualifications for making the business a success

As for the actual sources of funds—in addition to your own assets, relatives, friends, and acquaintances—the following are suggestions from SCORE:

➤ ***Consider getting active or limited partners.*** Active partners can or want to be involved on a day-to-day basis; limited partners supply expertise as well as funding but largely stay out of the picture.

➤ ***Evaluate bank, credit union, and SBA loan programs.*** Try the closest banks to your prospective or existing business first, because they are the ones that have the most interest in healthy and stable shops in their neighborhood. And be sure to take along your business plan, which banks consider the Bible for retail loans.

In an interview with SCORE counselors Tom Burke and Carol Seres at the Monterey Bay SCORE office, I asked for descriptions of buying plans, inventory control, and purchasing systems. Both Burke and Seres were in the apparel end of retailing, so they gave an example in those terms. However this example is applicable to any and every type of merchandise.

> The concept of a buying plan is "buying to your forecast." Your open-to-buy (or OTB) is determined by category (i.e., the number of tops to bottoms). Once you've made your initial buy, cash generated from sales then determines your subsequent OTB. The "forecast" is based on historic performance of each category.
>
> Inventory control is a guide to reports that you need for orders, and reorders especially. On a given day, February 1 for instance, you take your starting inventory and subtract sales, markdowns, damages, returns, and thefts, and the result is your OTB, along with the additional information of which items were good sellers and which weren't.

Inventory Control

As far as an inventory control system is concerned, Burke said that most shops today use computer software such as QuickBooks. But there are other types of software created specifically for certain categories of businesses, including tax-exempt charities.

As for your own financial assets, ask yourself these questions: Can you refinance a home or other real estate you own? How much do you have in savings? Do you need to sell some personal property? The answers to these questions show, in part, how serious you are about opening your own business and, in turn, your business plan will reflect this seriousness.

Licenses, Trademarks, Zoning, and Insurance

There are other need-to-know subjects you must explore for your plan. For example, a business license, state licenses, and a seller's permit or resale permit are mandatory. In addition, if you are not using your own name for the shop, you must register a Fictitious Business Name petition with the state, and in certain cases you may need to register the name with the United States Patent and Trademark Office. Also you need to find out zoning requirements and special requirements if food is sold on your premises.

Another need-to-know subject concerns insurance for your business. You need to discuss general liability insurance (including coverage for product liability and property damage if applicable) and business interruption insurance with an insurance agent. If you plan to hire employees down the road, worker's compensation is a must. But consult an insurance agent who specializes in business insurance. He or she can save you time and grief.

Taxes

For federal income taxes, you'll need to file a Form 1040 Schedule C if you operate as a sole proprietorship or Form 1040 Schedule K-1 if you operate as a partnership. You will also be responsible for Social Security and Medicare taxes. If you've hired an employee, you must also pay unemployment taxes. If your business involves liquor, tobacco, or certain other products, you'll need to look into the federal excise tax. You'll also need to file a state income tax form if your state requires one. Further, you may need to pay state and local sales taxes, county and city property taxes, inventory and/or gross receipts taxes, if applicable, as well as state withholding tax on employees, if you have any.

* * *

Good record keeping involves creating and storing detailed:

➤ Sales journals

➤ Cash receipts

➤ Checkbooks

➤ Receipts for cash transactions

In other words, you must have a record of *everything*.

* * *

As you can see, taxes alone make the whole area of bookkeeping a formidable process, so if you have no desire to set up your own do-it-yourself bookkeeping software, hiring an accountant is more than advisable. In fact, hiring a professional accountant or similar service is almost a necessity, and you must figure the cost into your business plan. The benefit of engaging an accountant/bookkeeper right from the start is that he or she will set up a bookkeeping system that is appropriate for your business, easily maintainable, and in compliance with tax reporting requirements—otherwise mistakes or tax penalties from incorrect bookkeeping and tax reporting could seriously undermine your finances and your business plan.

If you are not going to attend a SCORE workshop, at least send for all the materials you can, including the *Small Business Resource Guide* from the United States Small Business Administration and the pamphlet *A Small-Business Guide on How to Secure Financing* written by Goldhirsch Group, Inc., publishers of *Inc.* magazine, Boston, Massachusetts.

Gaspar Cardinale

Gaspar Cardinale, a semiretired longtime retailer who owned many shoe stores in the Monterey Peninsula area of California, has some excellent advice for new niche shop owners. Now a consultant, Cardinale can compare the present with the past, thereby offering well-rounded and comprehensive advice. I felt Cardinale was more precise than some of the other consultants with whom I spoke.

> The most important point for you to know now is that in these perilous, supercompetitive retail times, you must have enough financing today to subsidize your business for two years. The rule of thumb used to be a year, but no longer. Furthermore, you must figure into your costs income for yourself, for you must, of course, be able to live, if even frugally, the first year or two. Every spare nickel must go back into your business.
>
> It is imperative to have at least one line of bank credit but safer to have two—with two different banks—as backup for paying bills (at least one season of the year will

require more outlay than the others), along with the two years of financing in reserve. In order to have an edge up on competition it is necessary to start out with at least an ample inventory, increasing to an abundant inventory as quickly as possible.

Knowing that every category of a retail operation (i.e., apparel, shoes, hardware) involves an ideal number of "turns" per year, I asked Cardinale to define a *turn* (using a rounded figure of $100,000).

> Assume you have a $100,000 inventory—which you sell completely twice a year (which then totals $200,000 a year), you will have turned over your inventory twice per year—or, two turns yearly. And the gauge as to how well your business performs is measured in relation to other shops of the same type by the number of turns at those other shops. The ideal number of turns varies with different retail categories, so it's important to know what the average turns are for your category.
>
> Profits lie in achieving the highest number of turns which, in turn, means the number of reorders.

A strong believer in reorders, he told me he built success (whether it was through color, style, or whatever) of an item "with a winner, which you must go with until it is essentially sucked dry."

When asked about a return policy, Cardinale said it should be posted near the register as well as stated plainly on all receipts. Typically a return policy states the number of days a customer has to return an item and whether the store will refund in cash or store credit. Many of the shop owners who shared their customer service advice in this book have very liberal return policies because they believe it is essential to good customer service and repeat business.

Cardinale explained that credit cards, at least in larger stores, have replaced charge accounts because:

➤ Customers don't usually need to pay immediately. They have up to four weeks before that's necessary and even then they need to pay only a small portion of the bill.

➤ People generally want to acquire all the airline miles or other bonuses they can accumulate, so they have added incentive to use credit cards.

➤ There is too much paperwork with charge accounts, which means too much time and money.

Further, Cardinale recommends that a start-up business apply for, from its bank or banks, and accept every kind of credit card it possibly can as a means of payment from customers. Small shops or shops in small towns may still find it advantageous, even necessary, to maintain charge accounts. My own feeling is that it's mandatory to start with at least two credit cards—with the caveat that a few types of retail establishments are lucky enough not to need any because they are strictly cash-and-carry.

In terms of pricing, "Do not be greedy," is Cardinale's advice, and I agree with him wholeheartedly. It was the second or third rule I learned in business and I certainly had occasion, over and over again, to view the results of retailers who didn't heed the formula of acceptable markup: a going-out-of-business sign in the window.

There are formulas for markup in every area of retailing (e.g., apparel, gifts, hardware). There is markup on the high side as well as on the low side of a given formula. The high side is more acceptable if the quality of an item is of the highest caliber. But even then the markup can't be so high that customers are disgusted with what they consider to be gouging, for even if they love the merchandise, they often won't pay the price. Unfortunately, there are too many retailers who have considered their wares crown jewels and price their items accordingly. This seems to be especially true with antique shops. Nearly always, they buy their items at reasonable prices yet they don't seem to learn the adage: Do Not Be Greedy. If the price is right, or even slightly on the lower side, customers always feel they are getting value for their money—or even bargains—and will become repeat customers and tell friends about the shop.

As for markdowns, Cardinale says that timing is of the essence.

Know when to get into a market or trend, but also know when to get out. It is an unwritten rule that the first markdown at 30 percent is the most successful for the retailer. Recognize your hot item or fashion mistakes early enough that you take the markdown as quickly as possible.

We both agreed that when the item just *starts* to wane, it is time to take the first markdown; not at a measly 10 percent or 20 percent off—that means little to the customers of today who are used to shopping at discount chains. It is more profitable to sell at a medium discount in the beginning rather than a small 10 percent or 20 percent reduction, otherwise you will undoubtedly have merchandise left to sell later at 40 percent or 50 percent off. In other words, sell as much as possible with the first markdown, because your profit will be greater in the long run.

Cardinale had some more personal tips for new owners:

➤ When going into business, you must look successful but must be frugal in your lifestyle because all your money must go back into the business.

➤ There are four factors involved in a customer's purchase of an item, in order of importance:

1. Appeal (a customer buys with his/her eyes first)
2. Affordability
3. Desire
4. Need

➤ More and more, the trend is toward shops of one designer or one name (as in Coach, Tommy Hilfiger, SAS, Dansk, and St. John, to name just a few) because there is less risk and fewer markdowns.

* * *

To summarize, the more financially prepared and knowledgeable you are about starting your business, the more you can count on success. Begin your business/financial planning by contacting SCORE or any financial institution willing to give you free advice. Attend workshops if you need more information in specific areas of finance. Research the costs of a website and e-commerce if you plan to use them. Download free information from myriad online sources, such as business and trade magazines, or online bookstores that offer reprints of articles about finance, credit trends, taxes, bookkeeping, legal matters, specific licensing requirements for your state, and zoning permits for your town.

Success Stories

The Carmel Hat Company has created success within just 392 square feet of selling space. It sells hats and only hats—the right item, always at the right time (based on weather), in the right place, at the right price. During several unannounced visits I made to the Carmel Hat Company, customers crowded into this tiny shop at all hours of the day. The shop is in an area where a great number of tourists walk around. I noticed people entered in twos and threes, and once I saw a group of five people trying on hats.

The service is exceptional. The owners are Mary and Chris San Marćon, and on each of my visits to the shop, Mary spent time talking to each prospective customer, joking and laughing with them and asking questions of each. The sales staff is trained to fit a hat to anyone's head by adjusting or changing the headbands and making other necessary modifications, so sales are not lost by ill-fitting hats.

"To save space we created a stack-it-high attitude," explained Mary. Indeed, hundreds of hats are stacked high over the heads of the salespeople to save space, but still, on a busy day customers move sideways to get around each other. "Many times you go into a hat store and see one hat of this, one hat of that and only in one size and not a lot to choose from. But with almost every one of our hats we have each in all sizes; numerous, numerous hats in each style."

There are no window displays—only glass shelves sectioned off for piles of hats. Mary said, "Because the rent is so high here we cannot afford the luxury of lovely window displays. The hats are displayed where they're easy to see. We need to utilize every single inch of space." In a shop this size I wondered about inventory storage, and Mary explained that they use the 392-square-foot basement beneath the shop for storage. She also stores duplicates at her home. They carry about 50 styles for men and about 100 styles for women. "About 25 percent are my own designs, trim work, or sewing, and about 75 percent are imported from all over the world," added Mary.

The interior displays, high on shelves above the hats, are charming, lending an "old times" air to the décor, as do old photos that are hung wherever there's a speck of space. Adding elegance to the interior are intricately made hats from bygone eras displayed here and there on stands. The overall ambience of the shop is old-world European. Everything, even the soft music from a bygone era, contributes to the theme.

Mary does not use a buying office, but has many suppliers.

Over the years the suppliers have come to me, and they actually bring the hats to my home. We're honored as valued customers. I do attend (trade) shows so I can see the new things. There are buying markets in San Francisco and Los Angeles. And we have some "scouts" (friends) who find them on their travels.

One of her scouts recently saw a hat in Guatemala that is now being manufactured just for the Carmel Hat Shop.

Mary shared her own secrets of success:

You have to have a draw of people that is replenishable. In other words, we have the tourists and a location that allows a renewable source of customers. That's important. You have to have owner involvement (almost) all the time. You can't just hire others to sell or manage a store. If you don't have a hand in your business, you aren't going to be successful. So at least one of us is here. I'm the buyer. I know what I can sell. And I must fall in love with an item before I'll buy it and then I can sell it. It's one thing to hire employees and train them in all the tricks you know, but quite another to essentially turn the business over to them.

Service and a good return policy is very important. "If a customer returns a hat *exactly* how it left the store, it's always welcomed." The one service Mary does not offer, although she would like to, is gift wrapping, which is not possible due to space restrictions.

As to her inventory-control system, Mary said that she *knows* how many hats the store has at any one time and how many are sold. With so many years of experience and hands-on operation of the shop, I believe her.

Her advertising is word-of-mouth only.

I think my "secret" and what I'm most successful at is that I *listen* to people. My adage has always been: listen to the song of life. I listen to people who walk in the door. I size them up. Are they looking a bit down-in-the-mouth or not feeling good about themselves? Are they tired? Are they on holiday? Or a honeymoon? Are they trying to repair a marriage? Whatever I'm doing I listen. My husband says I give free advice with every hat. It's a listening process. It's not just about selling a hat, it's about learning what people want and providing something else in addition.

Mary related an anecdote about her free advice:

> One day a man came in and asked if I could help him. I thought he wanted a hat. But no, he wanted advice about his marriage. I asked him if there was hope left. He said yes but he didn't know *how* they could get back together. While we were talking he was trying on hats. He bought a hat and on the sticker that I attach to the inside of the hat, below the name of the shop, I wrote: "Anytime there's a problem in your discussion with your wife, put your hat on, take off all your clothes, stand before her naked and beg her to see you for who you really are." Because if you're naked you can't fight, you can't have an argument. Sometime after, he came back to tell us that his marriage was repaired.

The Carmel Hat Company is an excellent example of a "niche" shop: Hats, always in the right season, whichever one that might be, in abundant quantity, at the right price. It keeps prices as *low* as possible although quality is of the highest possible. And, of course, there's always Mary's good advice.

* * *

Henning's is perhaps the ultimate niche business—a special-occasion cake shop. I happened upon it as I walked by, glanced in, and saw five customers waiting. Five customers in a cake shop? Wayne Kjar, the owner, is a soft-spoken, quietly friendly, I'm-here-to-solve-all-your-problems sort of person who told me that his shop bakes an average of 30 special-occasion cakes a day with about 140 maximum (although when Father's Day coincided with some school and college graduations, he once baked 400 cakes).

For weddings, Wayne offers 12 cake flavors with 16 filling choices and four icing flavors. A range of two to six tiers and a staggering 27 sizes can serve from 40 to 400 people. All-occasion cakes come in 10 sizes serving up to 96 people. With these, Wayne offers seven flavors of cakes with a choice of 10 fillings, six icings, and six types of decorations. The baking area utilizes 70 to 80 baking pans of different sizes and shapes.

Among 19 bakeries in Santa Barbara, his is the only all-cakes shop. His customers come from all walks of life and from all economic and social strata. Asked what "all-occasion" meant, Wayne replied, "Everything from weddings to cat-and-dog-decorated cakes for a pet's birthday party."

It's no accident that 92 percent of customers are repeat customers. The shop's policy is to take back any cake a customer returns, even if it's not clear what's wrong with it, and bake a new one.

In an approximately 1,500-square-foot shop, which includes the kitchen, Wayne manages to display numerousmodels of cakes, wedding-cake toppers, bins of balloons, party favors of all kinds, and his latest addition (which takes up a large section of the shop), party goods. In response to customer requests, he now displays 34 party-goods ensembles—everything from plates of various sizes to table-cloths—in several different patterns, including animal prints. He even has a small area for the sale of rare party-size cake pans.

Wayne's father established Henning's in 1970, and Wayne, who has recently retired, told me that Henning's is one of only six or eight shops in Santa Barbara that have remained continuously owned.

Wayne's opinion is sought constantly by unsure, indecisive, unknowledgeable customers. He gently suggests, reassures, persuades; he's a born salesman. An appreciative customer said, "I work at Saks. We get all our employee birthday, shower, baby, and retirement cakes from here. They're delicious, the best in town by far."

When asked what he considers his greatest asset, Wayne said it is his employees. "I treat them very well with a lot better wages than other bakeries. I give them many freedoms such as time off, no explanations necessary, whenever they need it. They're part of my family." The last was said with pride, and the employees reciprocate with loyalty.

As part of his excellent service, Wayne will take back any cake a customer returns, even if he can't see what's wrong with it, and bake a new one. That's the reputation of the shop. It's no accident that 92 percent are repeat customers and 8 percent new customers and tourists. He offered some specific tips for prospective bakery shop owners:

- ➤ An all-occasion bake shop is the best sort of bake shop to open if there's not one in your town, because your business is all orders.

- ➤ There's no waste. You don't have to throw anything out, so there are no markdowns and no pilferage.

- ➤ Cakes are high-ticket items.

- ➤ Henning's is a destination-type business, so there's not a waste of time with "lookie-loos."

"Most cakes are carryouts with the only deliveries being wedding cakes," Wayne added. "And for those last two reasons, location is not important (certainly a plus factor) because it means you are able to rent in a lower-rent area. But parking *is* important." Wayne has access to two parking lots: one directly in front of the shop and one behind, in addition to street parking.

His secrets of success echo those of many successful shop owners:

> ➤ Be honest with yourself. That is, don't say you can do something you can't; be honest with your customers.

> ➤ Don't make excuses.

> ➤ Respect and listen to your customers.

> ➤ The customer is *always* right.

In the local phone book, I found a stunning color photo of a cake Wayne had baked and decorated with lifelike spring flowers and leaves. He told me that the yellow pages is his only form of print ads. But he also combines advertising and promotion at chamber of commerce events, trade shows, business mixers, and bridal fairs, where he offers a piece of a special-occasion cake to each attendee. Clever promotion.

One of his most unusual experiences was the wedding cake that never happened.

One day, an about-to-be bride came into the shop with her prospective groom. She thumbed through the photo albums showing just-married couples cutting their wedding cakes. She stopped at one, looked closely at the groom in the photo—it was her fiancé. He forgot to tell her he'd been married before! There were "words" that were still being uttered as they walked out of the shop, never to be seen again.

Wayne no longer features the bride and groom in the album's cake photos.

Another couple picked up a birthday cake for their young daughter but a short time later returned it. The cake was a disaster. The couple told Wayne, "Our chickens trampled all over it." They needed a new cake. Because Wayne's return policy is to offer a free replacement, he set to work baking and decorating a new one. Fortunately, there was enough time before the party started. Later the parents and sobbing child returned for the cake. Wayne handed the child a small white plastic egg that looked just like a real one. "Well, look what we found in your cake after the chickens walked on your other one," he said. The child's eyes got bigger and bigger and began to shine. "She really believed there was a special egg in her cake!" And this time there was a happy ending.

*　*　*

Many different modes of financing; many different ways to curtail expenses—as well as ways to spend—but all of these niche-shop owners are very successful. So take heed. Grab their ideas and run with them!

Kamal Debagamage has recently joined Hennings's management.

Chapter 6

Customer Service and Hiring and Training Personnel

A new business owner can do all the right things, fill out all the right business forms, stock all the right inventory, and yet still fail due to poor customer service. So it bears emphasizing that success and longevity depend on making your customers feel that your shop is the best in town to buy whatever niche items you sell, and to turn the majority of first-time customers into repeat business. In today's demanding society, where you are competing with huge conglomerates and discount chains, intimate, friendly, and personal service is the one area in which a small shop can, and should, excel.

You can accomplish this by following the advice of all the shop owners interviewed in this book, all of whom placed top priority on customer service, and by following some basic rules of retailing and training personnel.

The Primary Principles of Retailing

First, learn the primary principles of retailing until they become second nature to you. The first on the list is called The Golden Rule.

- The Right Item, at the Right Price, in the Right Place, at the Right Time.

- You can't be everything to everybody.

- Not every item will be a winner.

- An abundance of stock is a must.

- Do not be greedy.

- Your salespeople represent you and your reputation.

- Do not take for granted that your salespeople should know something.

- Listen, listen, *listen* to your customers.

- The customer is always right.

- Respect your customers.

- Be honest with your customers—don't tell a customer you can do something you can't.

➤ Don't make excuses to your customers.

➤ Be creative; use your imagination.

➤ Your marketing budget should be largest in tough economic times.

➤ There is only one chance to build an excellent reputation.

Learning the Ropes

There are specialized training courses in almost every aspect of retailing, including hiring and training personnel. You will find evening courses or weekend seminars at local colleges, SCORE chapters, through your local chambers of commerce, and by checking retail trade organizations on the Internet. In addition to learning about hiring personnel, you will also learn about their legal rights, your legal rights, tax-reporting requirements, and what types of insurance you will carry to cover accidents, worker's compensation, etc. Being knowledgeable about the legal aspects of hiring will give you confidence to hire the right people, whether they are full-time or part-time.

Are You in the Right Business?

When it comes to customer service, your staff should take its example from you. Are you sure you are suited to becoming a retailer, let alone making it your career? Because that is what it is: a career. Anyone thinking of opening a retail shop part-time or as a hobby is in for a rude shock, because it's not possible—owning a shop is too demanding of time, effort, and finances. So whether your personality is suited to selling (for the sales floor will be at least 50 percent of where you spend your workday) and whether the idea of selling something to someone intrigues, even excites you, or is *in your blood,* is of paramount importance to your success.

At this point in your research and development it would be beneficial to examine your motives and assure yourself that the dream you have is the dream you truly want. That may sound like an odd statement, but you have to assure yourself of the right answer before you sink yourself and your savings into a retail business where customer service is first and foremost. Who are you as a person? Are you outgoing? Do you *enjoy* talking to people? Do you have an agreeable personality? Are you curious about strangers? Do you have a liking for people as well as a tolerance for the long hours of working a retail week? Are you suited to tolerating the nitty-gritty of spoiled customers, rude customers, annoyed customers, angry customers? Affirmative answers to these questions are crucial, especially if you're going to be part of a one- or two-person sales force. Even if you employ several salespeople, it is mandatory for the new owner to sell at the busiest times of the day and week, to determine what sells, what doesn't, and what customers are searching for.

I've known dozens of retailers who not only did not have an easygoing manner toward customers, but responded to customers' questions with an indifferent answer and dour expression as well! Except in two instances where the superb merchandise spoke for itself—louder than the owners—all these retailers were out of business within five years, often much less.

When I first went into business with my husband, almost the first thing he taught me was: the customer is always right. Always. Research shows that every dissatisfied customer has an average of six friends to whom she or he will relate a bad (or very good) experience—and each of those six friends may tell six more friends—and if any of those people have had a bad experience, the tale will snowball. Suddenly you have the start of a bad reputation, and chances are you won't know why.

Hiring

The right salespeople must reflect the owner's overall attitude of loving his or her job: always enthusiastic, perhaps even excited by the merchandise, caring, helpful, resourceful, and knowledgeable about stock. In time, such employees become part of a loyal "family" and treat each other with warmth and respect. Your employees, in short, should know that they are caretakers of your business reputation.

As a new employer it may take a little time—and some trial and error—before you recognize good personnel and put together a loyal and caring staff. After all is said and done, hiring good salespeople will involve trusting your own instincts as much as anything else.

I've hired many, many employees and learned some valuable lessons about the *who* and *why* of hiring that I developed through the years. I found that salespeople—those who have experience in store and shop selling—are too often not the best help. Some no longer retain the enthusiasm for selling that they may once have possessed. Too often it's just another place to work; it's a "job" where they put in their time. Rather, I began to search for *customers* who were the most enthusiastic and would remark that they wished they could work in my shop instead of where they were currently working. Or they would say, "I love your merchandise and I'd love a job here, but I'd only have the hours when my children are in school," or they had other limitations such as only on Saturdays when their husbands took care of the children. Or they say, "I've never worked before but I love the shop and wish I could work here." They were marvelous candidates, and who better to hire? I would also be on the lookout for people who could attract their friends as customers: for instance, a young mother who knew several others and, with her enthusiasm, would be a live advertisement for the shop. They were some of the very best saleswomen I hired.

Another avenue I pursued to find the best candidates was to search in places I frequented: a waitress at one of my favorite restaurants turned out to be one of the best people I ever employed; so were a receptionist at a doctor's office and a secretary at a law firm—all of them needed a change from the type of work they were engaged in and a change of venue. I recognized their potential and promptly offered them a spot. They all became enthusiastic salespeople when they could handle merchandise they liked and could indulge in conversations with customers who were different from those they had dealt with in their former jobs.

One young woman I hired was the wife of an FBI agent who always seemed to be away on assignment. She was so grateful to be involved with something other than the charity work she had been volunteering for. Another, a recent widow in her early fifties, who had never worked, entranced customers with her Southern accent as I knew she would. Still another, a high school junior with top grades, was very energetic, always smiling, and extremely creative—she wanted to be a fashion designer. She was perfect for our juniors' shop—as were other high school students who would later go on to college.

They were all the right people for the right shop—and something more. They were all innovative: Why not create displays throughout the shop that tell a whole story, called a *theme*—from windows to individual displays? Terrific. I encouraged them to carry out their ideas, and the shop always benefited by their eagerness to be creative.

A star employee can increase the number of customers as well as the number of purchases. And even if that employee leaves, the customer is already hooked and will remain faithful to the shop.

Characteristics to look for during an interview are:

➤ An ***enthusiastic*** nature

➤ A ***positive*** attitude

➤ A ***smiling*** countenance

➤ A ***creative*** bent

➤ A ***helpful*** and ***alert*** attitude

A helpful attitude is the foundation, the core, of good salesmanship. Some employees are just order takers: they stand at the checkout counter waiting for the merchandise to be brought to them for payment and wrapping. Salespeople with this attitude are nothing more than "shop sitters," and what owner can afford such a costly indulgence? But then there is the salesperson who approaches a customer and engages in conversation to find out as much as possible about that customer's likes and dislikes. This gives the salesperson an idea of what drew that customer into the shop and what the customer is looking for: A gift? A collector's item? Something unusual? It also gives the salesperson a chance to casually show the customer an item or two. A good salesperson also knows when to leave the customer alone to browse after making sure the customer knows he or she is available for any questions or information.

When a customer says, "I'll take that," good salespeople will politely suggest, as they are wrapping the item, that such-and-such would "go so nicely" with the purchased item, or that the item has a coordinating piece to accompany it, in case the customer hasn't noticed it. More often than not, I found customers were grateful for the suggestion and purchased it. This is what I mean by a helpful attitude. Encompassed in that trait of a salesperson is a learned sales technique: the art of suggestion. To some salespeople, the technique comes instinctively. With others it needs to be taught.

Training

It is incumbent upon you, the owner, to conduct a training session in which you explain in detail about sales techniques as well as what you *expect* of the employee. Do not take for granted that he or she should know something. If you expect certain things, make those clear. Another aspect of training is the necessity of handling a phone inquiry well. With all phone calls the person answering the phone should convey warmth, enthusiasm, accuracy, and helpfulness.

Recently I had occasion to call an upscale kitchen shop to ask for directions. The place, I knew, was not easy to find. The response went like this:

"You know where the aquarium is, right?"

"Yes."

"Well you go up that street."

"What is the name of the street? There are two streets at that intersection."

"Uh, I don't know but you go *up*. You'll see the shop on the right-hand side and you'll see a small doorway. Go upstairs."

Now, she didn't ask me which direction I was coming from and, because of the shop's location, I needed to know the name of the street. The result of her unhelpful, unknowledgeable, uncaring response was that I never did go to the shop. Instead I went to its competition, and being in an expansive buying mood that day, I bought a couple of items—two sales at least that the first store just lost.

A friend of mine recently called a shop to ask if they still had a red dress she'd seen there and now wanted to purchase. She needed to know if they had it in her size. The answer from the order taker (one can't call her a salesperson) was:

"I don't think so."

"You don't think so? Would you check that for me?"

The order taker went to see if she had the size and was gone for ages. My friend, meanwhile, decided she'd call another store where she hoped they'd be more helpful and knowledgeable about their inventory.

How many potential customers have had the same experiences at these two shops and at thousands of shops around the country where salespeople simply don't give a damn? And, more important, do the owners of these shops know how their salespeople are handling calls? If not, why not? Why have they not trained their staff?

The best time for a training session, I found, was before the shop opened, when you can offer coffee and a Danish and encourage employees to let down their hair. Surprising ideas and suggestions can emerge from such a session if there is "take" as well as "give." A new and inexperienced owner can often learn from an eager employee.

*

When I was 15, not even a half year before I could legally work, I asked my father if he would talk to store owners or managers he knew to see if one of them would give me a job as a salesperson. He did, and my very first job was selling stationery in W.T. Grant's, a five-and-ten-cent store. I loved the job and was secretly in competition with the head salesperson to outsell her. So toward the end of August, when kids were buying back-to-school supplies, I had a checklist available of all the items they might need and I would rattle off the list to them. Rarely did they not add at least one item, sometimes more, that they had forgotten. If we had received a new item that I thought would appeal to them, such as a pencil box decorated with a popular theme of the day, I'd have that ready to show them and, invariably, if they could afford it (a bit more expensive than the usual basic pencil box), they bought it.

On my last day of work the manager of the store asked me into his office and offered me a job during Thanksgiving and Christmas vacations, for which he would give me a raise to 50 cents an hour. He told my father later that I'd "made better figures" than the head saleswoman.

When I arrived at the store in November, the manager informed me that I would be the head salesperson—the only one, I quickly discovered—in the gift department, their most important at Christmas time. I was really dismayed because the merchandise all looked so cheap to me. That first day I'd gazed at the array of gifts consisting of china and glass mostly, and though some items sold for as much as $20, I thought, *How am I going to sell this junk?* And then immediately thought, *If I didn't have much money and wanted to buy a gift for someone I cared about, what would be the best item I could find?*

Then and there I made a list, by item and price, of the best of the merchandise, but not necessarily the costliest. So when an uncertain customer approached me for help, I would ask questions about the person to whom the gift was being given and suggest the appropriate item on my list. I'd always suggest a coordinating piece if it were from a group of items of the same pattern, such as a gravy boat if the customer was purchasing a platter, for instance. Not infrequently, the customer purchased the extra piece (because I was careful to suggest a less expensive coordinate) with a what-the-heck-it's-not-that-much-more-and-I-feel-generous attitude. It was a valuable lesson. The challenge of selling something and then something more became fun and rewarding as I saw customers happy with their purchases. At the end of the season, the manager of the store offered me the job of manager of the gifts department as soon as I graduated high school!

I hoped I was presenting myself as warm and genuinely interested in my customers, for I loved conversation with them. Getting to know something about them and giving them the opportunity to reciprocate was the first secret, perhaps, that I learned about good sales technique.

A few years later, now married, but still long before owning my own retail shops, I was looking for a summer job during my pregnancy. There was a shop I had noticed—selling silver and pottery items—that attracted me like a magnet. The window display was so unimaginative and drab that I could easily envision how much more exciting I could make it if I got the opportunity.

The owner had little personality and was an order taker. He answered customers' questions only when asked, never volunteered to show them anything when they came in, and seemed oblivious to the demographics of his customers, many of whom were university students. He would hold a sale the day after Thanksgiving, which in any other area would have been a big sales day. But in that area the students had already left for vacation the week before! I knew that working there would be an interesting and creative challenge, and I persuaded him to take a chance on me.

After much resistance from him, I began trying out some new sales techniques:

➤ I trimmed his front window with a more diverse mix of items to attract new customers rather than just students.

➤ When a customer expressed interest in an item, I would use a small framed mirror or pieces of velvet on which to place the item and take it to a part of the counter where light would shine on it and it could come "alive."

➤ I found accessories for the customer to consider.

➤ When a customer purchased an item, I would ask the person to tell others about the shop.

Because my husband at that time was a medical student, I spread the word among our friends and their friends that a contest was going on: whichever student sent in the most customers would win a nice prize. The owner of the shop had no faith in this type of "marketing," so I had to offer to pay for the prize myself if my sales ploy didn't work. I really couldn't have afforded to buy a prize; I brashly believed that the new sales techniques would work. Fortunately for me, they did. The owner nearly tripled his sales figures within a few months. Not long after, he sold his shop, no doubt at a higher price than he had planned, based on higher sales volume.

My "education" in retail was expanding with hands-on experience, and I was learning what worked and what didn't. Of course, whenever I hired personnel for my own shops in the years to come, I always looked for that special spark of creativity and enthusiasm that had worked so well for me personally.

* * *

Training sessions need to include the subject of downtime, when the shop is empty and the salespeople have time on their hands. During downtime, personnel should attend to day-to-day chores such as "sizing in"—that is, putting each category together by size—which is important in apparel shops, as it can mean the difference between a sale and a walk-out. They should also dust shelves, clean glass items—especially important in gift shops to keep a shop looking perky as opposed to tired-looking. Unclean surroundings can be death for a shop.

Other responsibilities can include:

> Changing one or two interior displays a day, even though window displays are changed once or twice a month.

> Looking through customer requests, the guest book, and/or registries (bridal, baby, shower, engagement, housewarm-

ing, etc.) to see what needs to be followed up. For instance, if a customer wants an item but it is not in stock, a note should be made in a "request book." If that item is ordered, a salesperson or the owner can call and let the customer know it is now in stock. Following up on requests is a sure way to make and keep customers.

One training session is an absolute must, to be followed sometime later by a refresher session. When a salesperson is just starting, he/she is sure not to remember everything you say the first day, so plan a follow-up. It would behoove you to make notes of everything you want to talk about or teach the person so that you can, hopefully, use it for your next new employee as you expand.

Return Policies

As a new owner, you may be unsure how to handle returns. You and your salespeople need to understand the ramifications of a "good" versus "bad" return policy.

Have you ever been to a store where the employee gave you a hard time with a return and left you with a negative feeling about the store? And if it was the owner who presented a cool manner—not quite snotty, but just making it difficult in a way that left you feeling defensive—well, you wouldn't shop there again in a hurry, if ever. We've all had such an experience, and as the owner of the shop it will be your responsibility to make sure that never happens in your business.

Contrast that picture with one where the owner or salesperson, with no questions asked, gives you a credit card refund, a cash return, or a merchandise credit, pleasantly. You would be relieved—and impressed. It's understandable if, in a small shop, there's a "no cash" return policy, but even that can be explained to a customer nicely and sympathetically. Of course, your return policy should be clearly placed near the cash register or other area of your shop, and also printed on your purchase receipts.

I remember the first post-Christmas in my juniors' shop: During a Men's Night, a young wife whose husband had bought her four or five outfits, each of which we had beautifully gift wrapped, returned all of them. A teenager whose parents had bought an equal number of gifts returned all of those. I remember the dismay I felt in the pit of my stomach at the thought of crediting several hundred dollars. I also remember a lesson well taught to me: before handing back money or credit, try pleasantly, almost casually, to suggest finding the correct size, or different style, or a completely different item altogether. Amazingly, more often than not, with sincere help the customer winds up not only exchanging everything for other merchandise, but purchasing new items besides!

* * *

Taking a genuine interest in assisting customers simply cannot be stressed enough when it comes to training your staff. It was an emphasis that, like all other techniques I emphasized as a shop owner/employer, I first learned by being a salesperson on the bottom rung of the learning ladder.

In 1965, divorced, I was living with my three children in Westport, an affluent town in Connecticut. I felt it was time to go back to work for the first time in nine years. I knew, of course, that I wanted to sell but I didn't know where. Needing to buy a wedding gift one day, I drove to The Pottery Shop—the "in" establishment to buy gourmet goods, bakeware, kitchen gadgets, wine and liquor glasses, the latest in pottery dinnerware, and gifts for house or garden. Located on Route 1, not far from the center of town, the owners shrewdly banked on the fact that their good-sized shop with a large parking lot, which the main shopping area of Westport certainly didn't have in those days, would be a success. They were so sure of it, in fact, that they bought the warehouse-looking building with a definite plan in mind.

The buyer and co-owner of The Pot Shop, as we called it, was a former buyer of housewares and china for the most upscale department store in New York City, and she had all kinds of contacts and resources to buy everything off-price and in quantity. Therefore, The Pot Shop could sell everything for much less than regular retail. In addition, the owners created a chic appearance for the shop by maintaining a spare-and-bare look rather than a decorated one. This décor might be common today, but it was unique for the time—an intimate ambience that is difficult to create in an understated way. And the shop didn't offer gift wrapping, which was unusual then.

I was awfully nervous applying for that job, but the buyer had once been in my shoes and she offered me a job. Her one stipulation was, "Don't help customers, they prefer to help themselves until they need you to bring 12 or 20 of this or that to the check-out desk." In other words, be an order taker! Very difficult for me, who had always been service-oriented.

I would "sneak in" service when no one else was around. Then, however, I argued with the owners to allow me to make suggestions and show customers the merchandise to which I was referring. Well, I won in the end—especially after I pointed out the men who came in looking for gifts and appeared utterly bewildered.

One day a man strode in purposefully with an air of *I am used to instant attention.* I asked if I could be of service to him and whether I could make any suggestions about merchandise. He looked at me intently with piercing eyes and said: "I want you, nobody else, to pick out everything. To equip a kitchen for a cook and a dining room that seats 24. You will send 24 of everything for the table. Here's the address to send everything to." It was a Middle Eastern country, as I recall, and he thrust a piece of paper at me.

There was no time for me to ask one of the owners if 24 of everything was even possible. He handed me two $1,000 bills with a business card and said to call him if it cost more and he would send his driver with the rest.

I was terrified.

Ultimately, the owners had to buy a few extra items at retail from various other stores, and then they shipped it off.

What I haven't forgotten was the bottom-line price, including the shipping, which was $2,874 and some change. That was 1967. And the driver did bring in the extra amount due, in cash.

My point was further made after the owners saw a handsome rise in the Christmas sales figures.

How I loved selling gifts!

* * *

If your sales philosophy always emphasizes a positive attitude rather than a negative or suspicious one, you eventually become known in your community as being "the store to shop."

▶ Success Stories

One of the most interesting training programs I came across was at **Husk**, in Melbourne, Australia. The shop's owner impressively incorporate a very personal concern for their employees into their training and sales incentives.

The shop is also an excellent example of good general planning, merchandise, and employee training. Located on the trendiest shopping street in the downtown area, it encompasses 1,100 square feet, and was designed to give the narrow space the greatest depth possible and make it look twice as large. And it succeeds.

Justin Abrahams, the owner, opened this shop a few years ago, but he owns two others—one in operation for ten years, and the other four years—in the state of Victoria. His philosophy, he told me, is "to push retail design boundaries to their limits and to 'wow!'

Wall niches, recessed lighting, and minichandeliers highlight items in the Australian shop Husk.

our customers." And wow me it certainly did as I looked through the display window, with its huge earthen vase and cutting-edge hanging fashions, into the shop. I marveled at the incredible and different merchandise. I gazed first at a wonderful landscape painting on a wall, then down to the most fashionable sneakers on the floor, then over to crystal wine glasses like nothing I've ever seen before, and back to hanging confections of cocktail dresses.

With a Persian influence, the décor of the shop includes Parisian antique mirrors that run the length of the shop. While the lighting creates the ambience with its speckled spotlights that drop from the ceiling at uneven lengths, the wide, dark wood floorboards are a Husk signature. But it is the diverse mix of merchandise that really makes Husk unusual: womenswear, arts and crafts, and what Justin calls sensory care products—candles, soaps, and scents among them.

Although Justin originally had a strict policy of stocking only Australian products, that no longer holds completely true—it is now the concept of "everything natural" that is of the utmost importance. Justin will only sell merchandise made from natural fibers, whether it is clothing, home wares, art, ceramics, woods, or metals. He will only buy from designers who are young and passionate about their specialties, so he travels worldwide to find home wares, such as vases, bowls, and glassware, especially throughout Asia and Morocco. Still, about 85 percent or more of his merchandise comes from Australia. And as far as style, fashion, design, and price is concerned, the range is very wide.

The shop caters to customers from 18 to 80 years old; a mix of young adults, businesspeople, tourists of all ages, and students. One quarter are men buying gifts. To that end, explained Justin, he believes that the right salespeople are imperative. As part of his business philosophy, he offers a "Personnel Incentives Program" custom-tailored for each employee. And because he hires different personalities for different types of customers, one of the incentives is to pay for a course—educational, physical, arts, or crafts—each semester. "Any course that allows them to turn off work is the result we desire in order that our employees' personal growth and subsequent good health produce mentally healthy human beings. That, in turn, yields the greatest productivity and enthusiasm of the personnel when they return to work each day." The other incentive is extra money. Employees are assessed in two ways: sales, and keeping costs to a minimum (electricity and stationery, for example). These two factors are the basis of Justin's bonus program, a point system that translates into extra cash. A certain number of points are awarded for each "good deed," which accumulate and are rewarded at the end of the month.

All new salespeople must take a one-week course of "Husk Traineeship" as well as ongoing training programs throughout the year. "They are the lifeblood of the shops and we want them to reflect our values," Justin added, after I had mentioned how impressed I was with the two young personable saleswomen, one the manager, the other her assistant, whom I observed helping customers.

One assistant explained to me that they change the interior displays every day because they have "so many business people who come by at lunchtime that we need to constantly feature new things." Added the manager, "We have to change window displays at least twice a week because sometimes we sell an item the very day it's displayed in the window."

As far as advertising is concerned, Justin told me that he contacts magazines, or they contact him for articles, which is one form of public relations. He also stages events at the shop, where designers promote new collections or make their debuts. The press covers these events. The method he employs most for advertising materials is direct mail and e-mail.

Altogether, the unusual concept of the shop—the diverse mixture of merchandise, plus the excellent employee training—is accomplished brilliantly at Husk and creates an ambience that is as original as it is awesome.

* * *

In the small university city of Ferrara, Italy, near the Po river, is a majestic building that houses *Felloni*—a well-known fabric shop and smaller high-fashion men's boutique. Since 1961, brothers Alberto and Giulio Felloni, have owned the shop started by their parents in 1946. Felloni began as a fabric shop "with only one window." Their parents progressed to a shop with four windows and then to one with six windows. The current shop, Alberto proudly informed me, has seven windows, which are obviously extremely important to them for display purposes as well as for light.

Upon entering Felloni, I was assailed by a luscious fragrance permeating the high-ceilinged, 280-square-meter, airy shop. Alberto said the scent emerges mostly from the wood-paneled walls but also from the fabric. It evokes a feeling of warmth and hominess, he said. Alberto or one of the two salespeople greet customers in a manner that suggests they are honored guests in the Felloni home. It is an unusual and very effective trait because it is an entirely sincere, natural part of Alberto's exuberant personality as well as those of his mostly longtime salespeople.

The fabrics themselves are magnificent and include wool, silk, cotton, cashmere, alpaca, satin, and wool/silk combinations. They are also of the finest quality. Most are Italian-made because, as far as the brothers are concerned, Italian fabrics *are* the finest quality, "especially Italian silk," said Alberto. "But wool tartans and cashmere come from Scotland because you cannot beat their quality." The laces, antique and new, are so lovely that their display in the window was what drew me into the shop. Felloni's fabrics come in almost every shade of every color, but the reds and blues seemed to dominate.

The men's clothing boutique is a combination of designer and bespoke merchandise. There are handmade ties of every hue; shirts (almost all stripes) of every minute color variation, and bespoke suits, of which models are displayed on the lower floor. The brothers have created a niche of high-fashion menswear in Ferrara.

Alberto said his location "is very, very important. The street location is a reference point for tourists. Most tourists wander up and down it, so the window displays of Felloni's must be able to attract them, to bring them in. About 15 percent of our clientele is made up of tourists, but 85 percent are locals."

Alberto's best advertising is threefold:

First is the quality of the product itself. Second is the personal qualities of the salesperson. Third is the salespeople's awareness of the market—the current fashions and trends in style, quality, and color. We do not need to promote, to do events, because word-of-mouth is the best advertisement there is. Both in terms of the excellence of the product, that speaks for itself, and the extraordinary service we extend to our customers, which is well-known. We have a very good image and clients appreciate it and pass on the word. Our customers do the advertising for us.

The qualities Alberto Felloni and his brother look for and have in their salespeople reads like a manual of the perfect personnel:

➤ Greet the customers immediately with a warm smile and address them by proper name, always being courteous, constantly available, and aware that they want the best possible value for their money. Find their requested items no matter how difficult it seems.

➤ Pay attention to the market. Always be up to date on every aspect of our products, both present and future, by keeping abreast through printed materials and other means.

Alberto and his brother do not need to hold clearance sales per se, but twice a year they offer discounts and special prices on end-of-season merchandise.

A woman entered the shop while I was there, and the superb saleswoman greeted her warmly by name. The saleswoman then introduced the customer to the other salesperson, saying, "Marquise, let me introduce you to my new colleague," and mentioned the other salesperson's name. The customer wanted to purchase silk for a shawl. Alberto graciously excused himself from our conversation and went to greet the customer, whom I presume was at least a second-time client based on his inquiry of her family members, her dog, and her last purchase. Was she enjoying it? Did the accessories—embroidery and tassels that he had recommended—work well for the completed dressmaker-sewn garment? If she was not satisfied he would be delighted to exchange or refund any or all . . . and so on.

After several minutes, Alberto excused himself to cut a large piece of silk for a man with blond-and-gray dreadlocks, unshaven, dressed oddly—Italian chic, perhaps—and Alberto was as charming with the man as he had been with the first customer. He held a conversation with him until the transaction was completed, then bid him a warm goodbye.

What came to my mind was the scene in the movie *Pretty Woman*, where Julia Roberts walks into a snooty Beverly Hills apparel shop and is treated like dirt by the salespeople because she is trashily dressed. Later, when she returns to the store glamorously dressed to the nines, the saleswomen are falling all over themselves to help her, seeing just a big commission. But of course she buys nothing from them. I'm sure the salespeople at Felloni would die before doing something like that, and just as well, because the shabbily dressed man purchased some *very expensive* items! The lesson of Felloni's: Never judge customers by what they look like or how they are dressed.

The ambience of Felloni is extraordinary. The woody fragrance is sensational, but the warm and caring salespeople and their passion and eagerness to show you their lovely merchandise is even more sensational. In fact, the salespeople are more like hosts eager to show you their homes.

I regretted having to leave. To experience such a feeling is almost overwhelming—for a shop!

*   *   *

As I walked through the shops around the Du Pont Circle area of Washington, D.C., there was only one, a very small one, that I thought was outstanding: **Coffee and the Works.**

Coffee and the Works started 25 years ago as a coffee and kitchenware shop. Michelle Camden, the owner, bought the fairly new business almost as a fluke. The 450-square-foot shop is crammed from floor to ceiling with the eclectic mix of merchandise that she carries. She said she buys what she likes, but what she likes might be a completely different kind of thing than she's bought before. "I feel I must make a person happy and the item must have a function." She doesn't just like her merchandise and the mix, she *loves* it, and it reflects her personality.

The majority of Michelle's customers are twenty-something professionals, mostly businessmen and -women who entertain, and a substantial number of tourists—usually from the large Washing-

The majority of customers are twenty-something professionals and a substantial number of tourists.

ton Hilton three blocks away, who are in town for conventions and meetings. She said that doctors' and diplomats' wives and similar "well-heeled customers" buy more and in a higher price range. To stock such a variety, Michelle attends the New York gift shows twice a year.

Her product mix includes off-beat stemware for every type of drink, ceramic bowls, giftware, many types of exotic coffee beans and bulk teas, spices, chocolates, candies, candles, dinnerware, baking dishes, and a huge wall hung with kitchen gadgets and implements. All this is in addition to scores of other off-beat items of various sorts.

She creates her own interesting and fun window displays. She once had a window trimmer do them for her but found that she could make them more fun by doing them herself.

Her advertising is all word-of-mouth in the neighborhood, which extends two blocks south of the Circle and five blocks each way. Her street, Connecticut Avenue at DuPont Circle, is like Main Street. Customers use the shop as they would a small town general store or post office, stopping by to have a conversation with her, with each other, or with her employees.

"My greatest assets are my salespeople," she said. Through the years she has hired "attractive, nice, warm, very personable and friendly young people." Often they are college students, mostly women who are sharp, eager, enthusiastic, intelligent, conscientious, and who live in the neighborhood and were customers already. Michelle never has a moment's worry about them when she isn't in the shop, which is several days a week. She trusts them implicitly. She also talks fondly of them. Her employees, in fact, are one of her secrets of success.

Michelle related an incident about one of her star employees: She had been exhorting her salespeople to please, please sell the large, dusty, something-or-other that was taking up too much precious space on a top shelf. She herself had been unable to sell it. No sooner had she spoken than her star employee, a very attractive young woman who was helping a male customer at the time, climbed up the ladder, brought it down, and with a little flirtatious bantering, and a little convincing that this was the perfect gift he never knew he needed, sold it to him!

* * *

Velo Pro and Trailhead, located in Santa Barbara, California, are two codependent shops, although each could easily exist on its own. Each shop has its own name. Velo Pro, the bicycle side, has been in business for 16 years; Trailhead, the climbing and hiking side, for 10 years. Gregg, one of two Velo Pro managers, explained that people often combine two or more of those sports during a weekend (or longer) jaunt.

Situated on a corner that skirts the main street as well as an active side street, the retail operations total 4,200 square feet—1,800 square feet for the Velo Pro side and 2,400 square feet for the Trailhead side. They seem small, but in the latter case, light, bright, and inviting with many sunny windows. The location is perfect for these niche shops—not only the street location, but the scenic areas surrounding Santa Barbara are a magnet for the type of customers that Velo Pro and Trailhead cater to.

Velo Pro carries all kinds of bicycles for men, women, and children, from long-distance to mountain bikes. It also offers a complete bicycle repair shop. It carries everything one needs for mountain, road, and BMX touring: tools, parts, accessories, and apparel.

Trailhead is an unusual "hip" shop: it is a clothing and equipment outfitter for hikers, bikers, campers, and climbers, and it caters to men, women, and children. Trailhead stocks outdoor shoes and boots for trail running and hiking, casual wear, T-shirts, stoves, tents, knives, hats, sunglasses, wrist computer watches, books, maps, performance gear, baby carriers, and everything else necessary for backpacking and climbing.

But the unusual aspect of the shops-within-a-shop, the outstanding feature that impressed me the most (other than the unique nature of it), was the personnel. The sales people whom I spoke to, all men, impressed me with their tremendous enthusiasm.

"Everyone who works here has an area of expertise, is excited by sports in general and has his own specialty, such as hiking, in particular," said Ed, the co-manager. "Each employee also personally loves all of these sports, which is why they work here part or full time. Their enthusiasm is contagious." The shop's staff members organize hikes and events for themselves as well as for customers, and that's in addition to keeping abreast of the other events in the area. Furthermore, they are *very* involved with the community and with community service, such as the maintenance of hiking trails once every week. The shop maintains an event counter that offers, for example, trail maps for biking, hiking, and camping. They sell 200 copies a month.

The two-in-one shop has the most extensive advertising campaign of all the shops I've visited and probably the most traditional in that it pursues every type of conventional means available—and then some. The shops place coupons in the yellow pages—a full page with six or eight different coupons offering discounts for each of the three areas they promote. They also run radio ads and run print ads in the local "independent" weekly freebie. On cable TV they run ads in partnership with a cable company that, for instance, is locally televising the Tour de France.

The strictly utilitarian bicycle side and the bright and surprisingly cozy camping and hiking side make Velo Pro and Trailhead an amazing operation. They have the right items for men, women, and children, in the right place—a scenic area that is tailor-made for hiking, biking, and camping—and they stock items at the right time and at the right price!

Chapter 7

Marketing, Advertising, and Promoting

Understanding marketing will be a key factor in creating your business plan and your budgets for the next two years, so it is crucial to know the difference among advertising, public relations, promotions, and special events. (You will also find more marketing ideas for your grand opening in Chapter 9.)

Hollie Davies, who owns a marketing firm in Riverside catering to small businesses, shares the following marketing advice.

Defining Marketing

Marketing is a catch-all term that simply means getting your business out to potential customers any way you can. Strictly speaking, the advertising industry's definition of *advertising* refers to advertising that you pay for, whether it is in newspapers, radio, TV, Internet, phone books, or other areas. And public relations (PR) includes promoting you and/or your business by means other than buying advertising space—and there are many creative ways to do that. Promotions and special events are all part of good public relations, but often are referred to as advertising.

In an ideal world, you can hire a full-service advertising agency to help you promote your business. It will assign an account supervisor to work with you and then use in-house copywriters, graphic artists, and event planners to come up with a marketing program for your business. The advertising department will probably design your print, audio, or video ads for you and place the ads in newspapers, buy time on radio, and place your TV commercial on your local cable TV. If the agency is influential, it will get you the best spots for your money. You might be watching CNN or A&E at 6:30 one evening and all of a sudden your business commercial might pop on screen.

Media buyers try to choose TV channels with audiences that are most receptive to your niche product. If your niche is underwear for mature, full-figured women, for example, MTV would not be your first choice of channels. Likewise, if you sell pet rocks, you're not going to advertise on a food channel. Just as finding your location requires an understanding of demographics, so does marketing. You have to know the demographics of a radio station or TV channel audience in order to decide if it will be productive to advertise with it.

In addition, a full-service advertising agency will have a public relations department that will also be brainstorming ideas to promote your business in other creative ways. These often include special events and special promotions.

It sounds wonderful to have someone else do all this for you, but the drawback is that full-service advertising agencies are expensive—$5,000 to $10,000 a month is not unusual for a small- to medium-size business—and in the past decade or so full-service agencies have become few and far between. You might find one or two in a town if it's a tourist area where local attractions, hotels, restaurants, and businesses can support them, but these days the full-service agencies are mainly in large cities where they can be closer to major industries and large corporations.

With some creativity, however, you can plan your own advertising and PR program using some of the same ideas that would cost thousands through a full-service agency. Here are some tips that you can put into action with little effort.

Paid Advertising

Newspapers

Contact your local newspaper's sales representative and ask for the newspaper's advertising package. He or she will send you a terrific batch of information that will give you the demographics of the newspaper, its circulation figures, sample ads, specifications for placing ads, pricing, special offers, and much more. To pick up the slack of the disappearing advertising agencies, it is now common practice for newspapers to design display ads for customers free of charge. These can include photos and text, in color or black-and-white. You tell them what you want or send them a rough drawing, and they will design it, fax you a draft for approval, and let you make any necessary changes (typos and mistakes happen all the time). The size of your ad depends on your budget, but you can work that out with the sales rep. Also, be sure to ask if other shops in your shopping area already have a contract with the newspaper to run monthly ads. Newspapers often combine ads for several shops in a specific area on one page, with an attractive banner and snazzy advertising copy across the top of the page. They create individual color ads for each of the shops, put them all on one full or half page, and by pooling the ads, each of you saves money and attracts more customers to the shopping center.

Special-Interest Publications

Making the most of an advertising budget includes finding a "target" audience for your products. For many businesses this means advertising in special-interest publications—magazines that appeal to and are written for a specific type of reader. There are hundreds of these magazines, and a brief rundown of categories includes:

> ➤ Auto enthusiasts

> ➤ Business and finance

> ➤ Computers and Internet

> ➤ Entertainment and TV

> ➤ Fashion for adults

> ➤ Fashion for teens

> ➤ Floral

> ➤ Food and cooking

➤ Gifts

➤ Health and fitness

➤ Men's magazines

➤ Science and nature

➤ Sports

➤ Toys and games

➤ Travel and exploration

➤ Women's magazines

If your niche is toys or children's apparel, for example, you would want to consider running ads in magazines that are specific to children and parents. If your niche is gourmet cookware, a food or cooking magazine would be ideal. And if you sell collectible miniatures, you might consider advertising in a gift magazine.

Finding special-interest magazines is as easy as going to the Internet and using Google to find several hundred links in that category. As with all your other paid advertising, do a little research to see which magazines could be the best place to promote your products and your shop. When you have compiled a list of possibilities, view each of their websites, check their section on advertising costs, compare their circulation figures, and talk to their sales reps. Some magazines are weekly, some are monthly, and some are quarterly, but almost all require a commitment for a certain number of ads per year, and costs can run high. Have them mail you an advertising package so you can read it carefully and choose wisely.

When you advertise in a national magazine, it is, of course, essential to include ways for readers to contact you and/or have the ability to order long distance. Be sure to include your phone number, fax, e-mail, and website address, if you have one. And mention any additional services that you offer, such as doll repair, custom monogramming, smokeless candles, 100-percent satisfaction guarantee, or whatever you feel are good selling points in your particular niche category.

If researching special-interest advertising is too time-consuming, there are companies who specialize in doing the work for you. They can recommend target magazines, create ads, and do the paperwork. Charges for these services vary enormously. You can locate such companies on the Internet using key phrases such as "media marketing," "magazine advertising," and "special-interest magazine advertising."

Cable TV

Most cable companies now offer special packages for local businesses. The cable provider produces a TV commercial for you based on a contract for a certain number of spots on various TV channels for six months or a year. The commercial includes actors, music, and all sorts of professional technology. Prices vary, but these packages can be surprisingly reasonable, depending on where you live. Certainly they are more professional than trying to make a tacky, homemade commercial with amateur actors and bad photography. Contact your local cable TV companies, ask for their sales packages, talk to sales reps, and always compare prices and ask about any special deals they might have. Be sure to establish which channels your commercial will appear on, and at what times of day or night. An inexpensive package isn't worth a cent if your commercials are going to be shown at 4 a.m. five days a week when no one is watching. You can't expect to get 100-percent prime-time spots, but you must be assured of having a decent mix of times and channels. Get it in writing!

Phone Books

Paid advertising includes local phone books such as the yellow pages or business-to-business directories, which offer display ads for your business. They also offer special rates if you agree to buy a page of discount coupons. They will design the coupons for you, and you can offer whatever specials you want—discount prices, two-for-one offers, etc. Not only do local residents use coupons, many tourists use the phone books in their hotel rooms to find shops and coupons. Whatever promotions you offer in the coupons, be prepared to honor them for the full term of your advertising contract.

Put Yourself in the Movies

Some movie complexes have arrangements with promotion companies to run a one- or two-minute commercial for local merchants in the previews before the movie begins. Contact the manager of your local movie complex and see if he or she has this program available. The type of ad required is fairly simple, because it does not involve shooting a video. The theater can use a print ad that looks 10 feet tall on the movie screen and reads something like, "After the movie, stop by for coffee and sandwiches at Joe's Café, just two blocks from the movie complex." It doesn't sound like much, but when you consider that your ad runs in each theater in the complex, four, five, or six times a day, seven days a week for three, six, or twelve months, it's actually a lot of coverage. Introductory offers are quite low priced.

Websites: Individual, Co-op, and E-Commerce

Websites are, in my opinion, one of the smartest forms of advertising in today's marketing world. Potential customers around the world can find your shop with just a click of a button! And you don't even have to sell merchandise on the site for your site to be effective. Just having a worldwide Web presence, an eye-catching Web page, a map and directions to your shop, and contact numbers on your website will bring you business. Even on a basic website with no e-commerce capabilities, you should at least include e-mail capability so that potential customers can e-mail you with questions. That way, you can then contact them and mail them an order sheet or product list, and still do business. If you are in a tourist area, you would be certifiably crazy not to at least have a Web page, because today's tourists check the Internet before they leave home, looking for shops near their hotels and convenient ways to shop online.

You can research do-it-yourself websites through any Internet provider, or you can hire a local website developer to create one for you. A word of caution, however: website developers charge exorbitant fees for their work. Some are very talented and worth it, but others have little artistic talent and should not be relied upon to create a gorgeous or functional website for you. When researching website developers, be sure to see other websites they have created and talk to their previous clients for references. Also, decide up front who is going to maintain the site or update it. If you want to make minor updates yourself, say once a month to promote sales or special events, be sure the site is designed so that you can access it and that you know how. If not, factor in a Web maintenance fee.

Study websites that carry the same niche category as yours. You will find hundreds of individual sites, of course, but you will also find co-op sites that feature many different businesses—all with the same niche category—on one site. They allot one page for each business, and each has its own uniquely designed page, product list, pricing, etc. On the home pages of these sites you will usually see some form of this question: "Would you like to advertise on this site?" From there you can get more information and pricing. You will also see how your competitors promote their businesses. You can glean many good ideas from this research, but don't copy other sites; make yours special and unique.

Some major shopping centers offer co-op websites, where your shop will be included in a comprehensive website designed just for that shopping center. The site will include a list of all shops (with "links" to each shop's Web pages), photographs of each shop (interior or exterior), plus information about restaurants, parking, upcoming special events, and a map and driving directions to the center. A particularly good sample of a co-op website is sfbayshop .com. It lists information about San Francisco, East Bay, North Bay, and South Bay shopping centers. It features individual shop sites, lists e-mail contacts, and offers very pleasing graphics and design. Many of the shops included also have their own websites that include e-commerce capabilities, photographs of their product lines, and more personal customer interaction. In some shopping centers, inclusion in a co-op site might be mandatory as part of the lease negotiation, so it's best to check out any potential website costs or "extras" and factor them into your marketing budget.

No matter how small your business might be, e-commerce provides an Internet presence from which you can sell to a world market. But make no mistake, it is definitely paid advertising, because the cost of setting up and maintaining an e-commerce site can run high. You need to be sure that the results will, at the very least, offset any monthly costs, and at best—as you establish your site—become an important percentage of your overall sales and a profitable adjunct to your niche shop.

If you plan to have a website first and add e-commerce capabilities later, design your website (and the software that creates it) from the very beginning with that in mind, or you may incur the expense of designing a completely new website when you add e-commerce. It's a great idea to check out the e-commerce sites of major retailers to see how theirs are set up, and to make notes as to what e-commerce services you also would want to offer, now or in the future.

Thousands of websites offer information about e-commerce (see appendix B for a brief sampling). It's a daunting chore to wade through it all, even if you are Internet savvy. Getting one-on-one personal advice and referrals from other business owners who have had e-commerce sites for years—and have already compared services and prices—will save you many hours of frustration.

But do some homework first so that you understand, in general, what e-commerce is and how it works. Begin with the easier research, such as going to the websites of major credit card companies and Internet providers, and downloading or printing out their e-commerce information. When e-commerce began, the providers offered information that only techno-nerds could understand. But they have since become aware of how confusing their own information was, and continue to simplify their e-commerce information and set-up programs.

Type in "e-commerce providers" in your Internet search engine and you will find more than you could possibly imagine. Start with the major credit card companies, Visa, Master Card, Discover, etc., and Internet/e-mail providers to see what e-commerce packages they offer. The easiest to understand are often the easiest to work with. Compare services and prices. If you plan to sell internationally, you will need to be in compliance with government import/export tax regulations, so include those in your research.

Price should not be your main consideration; security and privacy for your buyers comes first. Packaging, refund policies, and mail or delivery services are all areas of "selling on the Web" that need to be planned.

In addition to researching e-commerce providers themselves, you can also find on the Internet the latest articles written about them, reprinted from most major newspapers around the world. Some sites offer charts comparing the services of e-commerce providers, but these are not always dependable, because some e-commerce–related companies put their own comparison charts together and, naturally, make *their* companies appear to be the best.

The good news is that once you have honed in on whichever company offers services you need at the best price, the set-up will be much simpler than the initial research. Most companies offer Web page templates in which you can just fill in your business's e-commerce information (and that's why your website needs the ability to easily incorporate e-commerce).

Once you have your e-commerce site set up, be sure that major search engines such as Google, Yahoo, AOL, and your own Internet provider's search engine can find your site.

Briefly, here is why search engines are important to the niche retailer. If a jewelry buyer in Minnesota is planning a trip to California to find new jewelry designers—whose work he or she cannot see at trade shows—the Minnesota buyer can go to the

Internet, type in "jewelry designers California" and come up with dozens of websites created by California jewelry designers. From that list, the buyer can explore each of the websites and contact the designers that look interesting. However—and this is important— if a California jewelry designer has a website that the search engines are not picking up, then its website will not appear on the buyer's initial list of search engine results. Just because you have a website doesn't mean you are automatically picked up by search engines. So to get the most out of your website or e-commerce site, do whatever is necessary to be picked up by *all* search engines.

Use e-commerce to sell, sell, sell. It truly is a sales door to the world.

Public Relations

If you have no budget for paid ads, PR is one area of marketing that business owners can do themselves. It's low budget and highly effective.

Newsletters

If you are handy with computers, you can create a good-looking one-page newsletter with word processing software (particularly Microsoft Word), plus a few tasteful bits of clip art, and a little practice. Or use the barter system and have a friend create one for you each month in exchange for some of your products. Keep your newsletter simple: promote upcoming sales, special in-store events, a photo of your employee of the month, new items arriving, a profile of a designer, etc. Keep it businesslike, not chatty and filled with useless articles, cartoony clip art, or items copied from other newsletters. Focus on information about your shop only. If you keep it in black-and-white, you can get hundreds of copies made for as little as three cents each. Just think, you are promoting your shop for just three cents per customer! What easier way to promote your sales and events to everyone who walks into your shop? Be sure your salespeople keep the newsletters by the cash register and hand one to each customer. (But don't put newsletters in with the customer's purchase in case the printing ink rubs off.)

E-Mail Promotions

Keep a guest book in your shop and invite customers to write in their e-mail addresses so that you can contact them with notices of upcoming sales. Customers who wouldn't normally want to leave a name, address, and phone number often don't mind giving out an e-mail address, because it is more anonymous. They're especially likely to give you an e-mail address if they enjoy sales and want to hear from you. A week before your next sale, event, or special promotion, e-mail all your customers with a short and welcoming invitation.

Press Releases

A press release is—just as it sounds—a notice to newspapers, radio stations, or TV stations of the who, what, when, where, and why of your event. Generally, unless you live in a very small town, the media does not send a reporter/photographer to cover grand openings or special events at a small shop unless something *newsworthy* is going to take place. A newspaper will, if space allows, include brief details of your opening in one of its sections—such as business, literary, or society—especially if the event is going to benefit a worthy cause. Include the following details in your press releases:

- ➤ Your name, the name of the shop, and a contact number or e-mail.

- ➤ What type of event it is (grand opening), and the type of entertainment included.

- ➤ The address, day, date, and time of the event.

- ➤ If your release announces a special event to benefit a charity or nonprofit group, include the name of the organization that will benefit from the event and what, if anything, is expected, such as canned goods for a "feed the needy" charity, wrapped toys for a children's charity, a small donation for a museum charity, etc.

When you pay for advertising, you get to dictate when and where you want your event promoted. But with free coverage it is not the media's obligation to include your news. You will not create goodwill if you approach them with the attitude that your news is earth-shatteringly important. If you learn how the media works and understand their limitations, you will make friends and get far more coverage of your business in the years to come.

Flyers

You can create attractive flyers in color or black-and-white and post them on community bulletin boards or wherever flyers are allowed.

Always keep a stack of flyers at the checkout desk when you are promoting upcoming sales and events, and offer one to every customer.

Writing Feature Articles

If you have a great deal of experience in your chosen specialty and are able to write well in a journalistic style, consider writing an interesting article for a trade magazine on a topic pertaining to your niche product. When I worked as a copywriter for advertising agencies, I wrote dozens of feature articles for agency clients. I interviewed the clients to gain facts and information for a good story, biography, or corporate profile, then wrote it for them. Naturally, my name didn't go with the article; the client's name and photograph were used, and the articles were placed in appropriate trade magazines or even nontrade magazines. This is standard practice in PR agencies. So there is no reason you cannot do the same for yourself. Magazines don't often pay for these trade articles, but it's wonderful publicity for your shop. Keep the article short, about 600 words max, and make sure it's a topic, or a new angle on a topic, that hasn't already been written about (read back issues of magazines to see what topics they have covered, or check their websites).

You can call or e-mail editors and see if they would be interested in the topic, or you can just write it, submit it, and hope for the best. Be sure to send a cover letter saying you are not expecting payment. Sometimes editors will call and say they like the article so much they would like you to expand it. If it is published, you can place reprints of the article, nicely framed, in your shop or in other promotions, and of course in your newsletter. You might also consider doing the same type of article for a local newspaper. But only do this if you are sure you are a good writer; a poorly written article will do more harm than good.

Customized Logos

If you can use a word processor, you can create a logo—even if it's just the name of your shop in an interesting or unusual font (typeface). Have a local print shop enlarge it and use it to imprint your shopping bags, gift wrap, or even T-shirts. If you are creative, you can probably come up with a really attractive logo, and if you aren't, have a local graphic artist design one for you for a set fee, or exchange product for a service.

Promotions

To follow up on Hollie's advice, here's some of my own. Different promotions have different goals. The usual promotions are percentage-off sales and perhaps a two-for-one type of promotion. The more imaginative ones take thought and effort to arrange. For instance, if you own a bookstore, why not inquire about local authors who can host discussions about their latest books? If you own a sports shop, what about presenting a demonstration by an exercise guru, especially if he or she is local? How about engaging a manufacturer's representative to talk about current fashion and style in your apparel shop? You could also host a "trunk show" (samples of the next season's collection of a particular designer or manufacturer). All of these would be accompanied by a reception with wine or refreshments (research local wineries, if there are any, to inquire whether they would do a free tasting) and cheese or dips and crackers.

Other types of promotions include drawings for free lessons, part of a wardrobe, a book, a pair of champagne flutes, a vase, or any item as a giveaway. The drawings may or may not require a purchase. Collections of food or used clothing for the Salvation Army some weeks before Thanksgiving or Easter will prove you are community-minded but will also bring in customers during a slow period, perhaps when new merchandise is just arriving. The same types of collections for local, state, or national disasters will also give you positive publicity in newspapers, on the radio, and maybe even TV, in addition to the satisfaction of performing a community service.

The more events you can arrange, the more names you will add to your mailing list, the so-very-important goal in your first few years in business.

What are events? They are everything to do with appropriate-to-your-business appearances in your shop. The purpose of events is to increase your sales, so the more potential customers you attract the better. A jazz duo in a sports or hip apparel shop, a violinist in a gift shop, an artist sketching people in a stationery shop, a trio in a book or music shop, a guest chef or local cookbook author in a kitchenware shop—the possibilities are endless. All it takes to dream up an event is imagination.

Other types of events include a Christmas-in-July event (which we found to be very successful; lots of giveaways saved from Christmas), a how-many-pennies-(or candies)-in-the-bowl event, at which a not-inexpensive item is the prize. There are all sorts of events for which prizes are given away.

One of the most successful of all events is customer appreciation day. Talk it up with every sale. Most often it will be your anniversary event, but not necessarily. Arrange for a photographer to take free photos of your customers against a funny or beautiful backdrop with your logo on it (great advertising). Have on hand trays of sandwiches (make them yourself to save money), a choice of sodas, and small packets of cookies. Offer a percentage off any item bought that day, and a free but useful small gift such as a tiny flashlight key chain with your shop's name imprinted on it (another advertising opportunity). Be creative, use your imagination. The ideas for such a day are limitless.

In-Store Promotions

Just as I created a highly successful Men's Night in one of my shops (see Chapter 2), you too can plan special events in your shop that will bring repeat customers and new ones into your store. The event should relate to your niche. If you sell beauty products, offer free makeup classes; if you sell books, have a monthly book discussion group; if you sell plants, have a gardening expert hold a Saturday-morning advice session; if you sell apparel, hold a fashion show; if you sell children's items, have a story-reading time every Saturday morning (while the kids are enjoying the story, the parents can shop). The ideas are limitless. Promote the event by putting up flyers on local bulletin boards, placing paid ads if you can afford it, writing it up in your shop newsletter, e-mailing your customers, or by using free event-promotion space that most newspapers offer—whatever way you can spread the word. Ask nearby shops if they will help you promote your event. If customers at your store will have to pass their stores, it's good business all around if shops cooperate with each other as long as they don't carry the same goods. (See Chapter 8 for more ideas and examples of in-store events.)

Theater and Other Event Advertising

A seemingly unusual place to advertise is in programs at local theaters, concert halls, or sports centers in your city or town. It's an excellent venue for art gallery, bookshop, stationery, travel, and gourmet-food shop advertisements, particularly. A program affords great exposure because there are so few ads and so many captive readers. This I discovered several years ago when I started a travel consulting business in Los Angeles. I was able to afford one ad each month in just one well-placed source. After a great deal of research of just about every newspaper and magazine in the area, I concluded that *Playbill* fulfilled my need and reached the customer base I was searching for. It was the appropriate venue for my business.

In other words, advertise where it's appropriate for *your* business.

Charity Benefits

One of the nicest ways to combine public relations with a worthwhile cause is to donate merchandise to charities, to be auctioned off, sold, or given away. Check your newspaper for any upcoming charity events, or contact charity organizations in your area and offer to help them. Depending on the charity event, a contribution can reap excellent promotion. But even if it doesn't, you'll feel better for having done a good deed.

Gift Wrapping

It can't be stressed enough how important gift wrapping is. Just as designer jeans are a status symbol, so too can be the name of your shop printed on bags and boxes, especially if you have designed an unusual logo. Remember, a logo can be one of your most outstanding symbols. Likewise, gift wrapping can show off this logo. So few shops offer it anymore, and if they do it's too often uninspiring and unidentifiable. Too many owners don't understand that gift wrapping is a form of advertising. You want people walking down the street to see a package with your logo on it and say, "Ah, the so-and-so shop does gift wrapping. I must remember that next time I need to buy a gift." Shop identification is the goal of this type of advertising. Include these in your advertising budget, especially if it increases your ability to purchase more outstanding, more identifiable supplies. As for the cost of gift wrapping: one type, your basic wrap, should be included in the budget, but if you offer other types of paper and ribbon for weddings, showers, anniversaries, and the like, you can charge customers for the cost, plus a slight profit.

With respect to your marketing budget, there are two points to remember. The first is that your budget should be largest in bad economic times—not in good times. Logically, it is in a recession that you need to draw new customers into your shop; they will be there when the economy is good anyway. And the second point to remember is that you build your reputation within the first several years. You have only one chance—those first two or three years—to accomplish that. So use every dollar and every idea you can for advertising, promotions, and events. By the fifth year, if you can give yourself an E for Excellent Effort, you are already successful. If not, your future looks doubtful.

The Best Marketing

For any business owner the best marketing involves no paid advertising at all, and that should be your goal. Strive to make your business and customer service so outstanding that word of mouth will bring in all the customers you need. What you save in costs will go a long way toward improving and expanding your inventory and upgrading your shop!

▶ Success Stories

Scabass is an incredible French shop that excels in the new age of advertising, public relations, promotions, and events. It is a corner shop on a small side street in Paris with a display window so captivating that it was easily the most outstanding shop of many, many in the St. Germaine district of the Left Bank. It was outstanding because the gown in the window epitomized what has come to be known as original Parisian Chic. Observing the scene inside, I was struck by the beaming facade of a salesperson, Séraphie Chaine, whom I later discovered was one of the two owners. Her partner, Elfriede Facchin, is the other designer of women's clothing that the two refer to as "creations."

Mi & Canna is the resulting label of a network of many freelance artists and craftsmen who are involved in the creations—an association of painters, photographers, weavers, and embroiderers whom Elfriede and Séraphie call upon to create unique designs, fabrics, shapes, and colors. They are all engaged in a new and different form of art—"alive or living art" as the owners call it. Because of the amount of work involved in a single unique piece, each piece costs $5,000 to $7,000.

The dress presented in the Scabass shop window was designed by Mi & Canna in collaboration with the Spanish artist Charo Marir, who created the fabric from one of her paintings.

The partners divide their business into three parts:

1. One-of-a-kind couture pieces such as wedding gowns or ceremonial gowns and dresses inspired by a theme or event.

147

2. The day-to-day collection, consisting of several lines of "street wear" (interchangeable for daytime and nighttime). It is the outgrowth of the core creative elements of the couture pieces. The lines consist of jackets, pants, tops, skirts, and dresses, in all sizes at moderate prices.

3. A range of unrelated items that they call Coup de Coeur, such as T-shirts, interior décor pieces, and a range of accessories at very affordable prices.

Elfriede and Séraphie began their original niche business with other lines, and five years later they eliminated those other labels and presented only their own Mi & Canna lines and label. Séraphie said that the business has changed almost completely from their start-up beginnings. They used to be their own bookkeepers, with an outside accountant, which is no longer the case. She added that it is *very* difficult for a start-up to get a bank loan in Europe, and especially so in France. Also, raising funds from friends, families, and interested outsiders is not an easy task.

On the subject of personnel, she said, "We hire only those who understand our concept and are compatible with it, whether they are salespeople or artists and artisans. We emphasize that there must be confidence and trust in each other's personalities and ideas."

Séraphie informed me that they don't advertise in newspapers or use other traditional methods of advertising.

We are one of 10,000 shops, so it would be useless. Our customers are scattered all over the very large city, so that traditional ways of advertising might not reach them. Old ways of doing business are changing rapidly so shops must adapt quickly to new methods by remaining flexible, and

not be afraid to implement new ideas and concepts of man-
ufacturing and selling.

To this end, Scabass adopted a method of advertising by e-mail.
This accomplishes two purposes, and timing, Séraphie feels, is important. When she and Elfriede planned to eliminate the extra
"outside" labels they no longer wanted to carry, for example, they
e-mailed their client list "only a few days before the event, to create
a dynamic of surprise." E-mail, she told me, is now used for all
events and promotions, and sent only a few days before the event
so people won't forget it.

For purposes of advertising their couture collection, the owners
phone the appropriate people at newspapers, TV stations, radio stations, and magazines. The media will always cover the shop's
unique creations because those creations are designed for specific
celebrities and socialites who are attending charity events or weddings of other high-profile people. The partners use a theme, which
they present to the press, because the shop needs "the right image
for the right media." In addition, TV presenters (anchor people)
and celebrities wear a Mi & Canna creation for special events on
TV.

Séraphie and Elfriede also use a theme to plan one event a
month for their clientele and their friends. One month it might be
weddings, another month it might be the presentation of a new
artist or craftsman, or perhaps a Feel-Good-About-Yourself party.
They hold these marketing events in their intimate downstairs
showroom, which is comfortably furnished. They also use this area
for teas and fashion shows, musical soirées, and art exhibitions of
the many designers on their payroll.

Although she is now highly experienced in her business, Séraphie has not forgotten the early days of opening her niche shop:

149

Only one month after the launching of the Mi & Canna label we were invited to the Cannes Film Festival. On the last day of the festival, for the award ceremony, we had created just one dress especially created by our main designer and an Algerian weaver for that festivity, and taken along a few other dresses. It was 10:00 a.m. and we still had no one, let alone a celebrity, to wear the beautiful dress.

We went to the Festival office and, suddenly, a famous French actress arrived to pick up her ticket for the evening. We took this opportunity to present our work to her and she was so impressed by the beauty of it that she said she must wear it. But we needed her to try it on to make any necessary adjustments. Time was too short to go back to the hotel for the fitting, so our only solution was to undertake the fitting in the ladies restroom.

In the meantime, three young actresses appeared in the office hoping for an extra lucky ticket to walk down the red carpet. They didn't take their eyes off the extra dresses we had brought along, so we offered to let them wear the dresses for the award ceremony. They were thrilled. About 4:00 p.m., we gathered all the actresses together to start the make-up session. Everything was fine until we received a phone call telling us that there were no tickets for the three girls. We called everyone we could think of, but it seemed that tickets had been reduced for security reasons, and the entrance would be tightly controlled. Now we had four beautiful actresses and only one ticket!

We were in a panic. What to do? We decided the only thing we could do was give it a try, and we said to the ladies, "Go for it! Go as if all of you have tickets and let's see what happens." We were really scared because once you climb up the stairs to the theatre and are rejected by a security check, the only way down is right in front of hundreds of TV cameras from all over the world and everyone would see them rejected. What humiliation that would be. But we trusted our lucky star.

The Mi & Canna limo pulled up at the event, the four actresses climbed the stairs to applause, and the four ladies went through the entrance with no problems. They were such an incredible group of ladies in those gorgeous dresses that the security people forgot to ask for tickets!

*　*　*

The Book Den is a 2,600-square-foot shop located a few doors from the main shopping thoroughfare in Santa Barbara, California. Eric Kelley owns the shop, which does not look at all like a typical used-book store—it has the look and feel of an intimate, paneled library in a private home. That was my first impression as I stepped through the door. I was amazed when I found it to be a secondhand bookshop, many of which I've seen, and none looking even remotely like a private library. It was carpeted and had a huge glass-fronted bookcase against a wall on one side of the door. An exhibition of local artists' paintings hung from the high ceiling on both sides, and the space was softly but dramatically lit, with skylights providing additional natural light.

Only after gazing down the spacious aisles for ten minutes, puzzled, did I realize the walls were, in fact, painted brown—not wood at all—and large air ducts were running from front to back. So clever was the lighting, with its hanging shaded lights, that the ducts were almost obscured. The other factor, besides the lights, that gave the appearance of a library was the antique rolling ladders, once found in neighborhood grocery stores, hardware stores, and libraries, to reach the top shelves of high-ceilinged rooms. The owner had the shelves constructed to accommodate the ladders.

Eric Kelley likes selling; he likes selling books. He is a personable man with tremendous curiosity. He soaks up every bit of information his customers utter. He is a man who loves to learn. Asked how he got into the business of used books, he replied that after college, a job as shipping clerk at Barnes & Noble familiarized him with book titles, which naturally led to his curiosity about the books. One year later, he became a book buyer. Four years after that he'd had enough, so together "with a burnt-out concert pianist," he moved to Santa Barbara and took over a small book shop. He and his partner moved to a larger shop next door, his present location, in 1990. Eric bought out his partner and has been the sole owner for 25 years of the bookshop's 102-year existence.

"People think books are so important they can't throw them away. So they keep them, then give them away for pennies just so they find a loving home," said Eric.

Eighty-eight percent of Eric's customers buy used books, 10 percent buy from the website or from the remainders pile (bargain books), and 2 percent buy promotional books. Seventy percent of his customers are walk-ins; 30 percent buy through his own website, amazon.com, and other sites. It is the online customers, Eric implied, who make the business so successful. "We will also take books back within a week for store credit. On mail order sales we give money back."

A male visitor from Bloomington, Indiana, visits the area with his sister every year and always makes his first stop The Book Den because "it's the best used bookstore I've ever seen." His special interests are travel narratives and art books. "As a used bookstore it's very well organized with an excellent selection of the subjects I'm interested in."

Another customer, a Santa Barbara resident, said: "I like the atmosphere. It's small enough to feel cozy which is what I like about libraries. This shop, in fact, feels like a library and it's set up the same way."

Eric advertises "only where people look for my type of business, in the yellow pages of the phone directory." Here are some of his secrets of success:

- ➤ Get to know the gossip columnists from the local papers. They need to know who you are, because more needs to be known about you as an owner of a used-merchandise business.

- ➤ Market yourself to those who are in a position to market you to others.

- ➤ One must earn the right to be known, which means volunteering for good works in the community such as Friends of the Library and community advisory committees of various sorts; eventually, become chairperson of at least one.

As for promotions, Eric attends art receptions because he gets "a certain readership out of them," but he also stages exhibitions and receptions of local artists' works, which explained the exhibition hanging in the front section of the shop as well as in the window displays. He is also an integral part of the Santa Barbara Book and Author Festival held once a year in September.

Eric's greatest asset, he believes, is acquiring as much knowledge on as many subjects as he possibly can—and with his great natural curiosity it is a pleasure for him—in order to be able to speak to customers knowingly. But, of course, he learns from his customers as well.

One of the many interesting incidents he's experienced concerns a copy of a seventh printing of James Joyce's *Ulysses*, which is valuable because a seventh printing is the first printing of a book (which is allowed) to have revisions to the text. "The book was originally published in Paris with 'paper wrappers' but this copy was rebound in purple leather. Really ugly purple," explained Eric. "It was priced quite high. A wealthy customer came in and bought it, not because of his love of Joyce, or because of its value, or even because of its status as a seventh printing, but because he was putting together a purple wall of purple things in his library!"

Eric Kelley believes that used books is a good business to get into, as long as it includes an Internet business from the beginning, because that can be lucrative.

*   *   *

Glancing through the display window of **L'Atelier**, a yarn shop located on a corner of the trendiest street in Santa Monica, California, I was struck by the coziness of the scene within: several women sat knitting and chatting around a table. Inside, the shop was bright, cheerful, charming, homey, and colorful with its various hues and shades of all types of yarns. It seemed more like a private club of friends, because the owner and salespeople chatted with the customers, whom they addressed by first names. It is, in fact, exactly that warm ambience that Leslie Stormon and Karen Damskey set out to create when they opened the doors of their second shop 13 years ago. Karen was the original owner of L'Atelier in Redondo

Beach, California. The 775-square-foot Santa Monica store and the Redondo Beach location share the same goals and ambience.

Leslie and Karen feel passionately about their shops and knitting. Leslie told me that some of her customers, who suffer from depression or serious physical conditions, or are on chemotherapy, have been taught to knit and now find the activity to be a form of meditation. It is certainly understandable, because Leslie acts as a kind of healer. She and her staff are always eager to teach these sufferers the technique of knitting, in hopes that they too will find relief. Leslie emphasized how much fun and humor they all share with their customers and that the goal of the extraordinary collaboration of the two partners is "to change the image of knitting and how people think about it."

L'Atelier is not just a yarn shop. It is a complete knitting shop that sells almost everything one might need to complete an item for a man, woman, child, or home. It sells yarn from all over the world, plus all sizes of needles and an unusual stock of buttons.

Among their many innovations over the years, the two partners have:

➤ Designed and imported many of their own yarns

➤ Created original patterns for most of their clientele, for such items as sweaters, coats, blankets, and just about anything a customer requests

➤ Started a knitting club years ago of which there are now over 1,500 members worldwide, all of whom pay an annual fee to belong and are entitled to such perks as discounts on designer yarns, three original designs every month, automatic book subscriptions, an archive scrapbook, and complimentary patterns

➤ Created a website of all their offerings

➤ Printed a monthly newsletter for customers and club members that included a sweater pattern-of-the-month packet, new designs, and the latest yarn samples and color choices, with a bit of philosophy thrown in

➤ Printed a yearly 42-page direct-mail catalog

They do some advertising exclusively in knitting publications, but "L'Atelier is so well-known that word-of-mouth is all that's necessary for local business," Leslie said. They also promote and host a "trunk show" of a yarn company's new yarn samples, sample sweaters, or other items.

Leslie emphasized that everything in the shop is of the best quality only, and that she and the staff provide unusual service. Whether it is guiding a customer through a problem on the phone in Idaho or sitting down at the knitting table to teach a new customer how to knit, everyone who works at the shop gives as much personal service as possible. Karen and Leslie treat their personnel, who for the most part have been with them for years, as family. It is a close relationship between the owners and customers. Karen and Leslie are always trying to entice new young people, particularly, to knit. And by "people," Leslie emphasizes that there are several male customers as well.

On the subject of buying, Leslie said sales representatives come to the store but she and Karen attend trade shows on both the West and East Coasts, as well as Cologne and Florence, to view the latest styles, colors, and designs.

Leslie has simple advice for newcomers to the niche business:

➤ Have lots of money available for cash flow.

➤ Love what you are doing.

➤ Don't take criticism personally.

Her favorite shop story occurred a few years ago when a lady drove into the parking lot outside the entrance of L'Atelier and drove right through the display window of the shop! Police were summoned and the lady said to them indignantly, "If the owner had a larger 'Closed Monday' sign, this wouldn't have happened." Her Jaguar went six feet inside the shop. The city building department red-tagged the premises, which meant no one was allowed to enter for a few days, even Leslie and her staff. Never ones to let such setbacks get in their way, Leslie and Karen set up shop in the parking lot with the undamaged merchandise, complete with tables, chairs, and umbrellas. Through rain, heat, and cold they carried on business that way for the next eight weeks!

L'Atelier exudes a happy atmosphere. The attitude of Leslie, Karen, and their staff toward their customers is: let's get to know each other personally and have fun!

* * *

The Carmel Doll Shop is a world of enchantment, like walking into a 400-square-foot dollhouse filled with antique dolls, dollhouses, and doll clothes. The other-worldly ambience of the shop is enhanced by unique displays that, interwoven with one another, produce a world of magic in this niche business.

The shop is located on a street where tourists are not apt to explore, and this is the perfect location for this shop because the owners, Michael Canadas and David Robinson, are not interested in lookie-loos—the merchandise is too delicate for careless fingers. The spellbinding inventory is purchased worldwide from estate collections or at auctions. Carmel Doll Shop is an excellent example of offering services related to the products sold in the shop: A "hospital" for doll repair, dollhouses, and doll clothes, plus alterations. Dresses, skirts, blouses, slips, wraps, shoes, and accessories of all kinds fill drawer after drawer, and these antique creations are hand-sewn using the finest linen, wool, silk, lace, and cashmere.

The Carmel Doll Shop offers services related to the products sold in the store, including a "hospital" for the repair of dolls, dollhouses, doll clothes and alterations.

Michael Canadas himself is an excellent promotion for his own business—he is a world expert in the field of antique dolls, giving lectures and presentations at doll shows and conventions, and writing articles for doll magazines. Advertising takes the form of ads and articles in trade magazines and mailers targeted toward collectors rather than the general public. In years past Canadas attended doll shows worldwide, carrying dolls aboard the plane with him. But because of 9/11, new security laws require that the dolls' intricately wrapped boxes be unwrapped, and the process of rewrapping is too complicated to make this feasible. Therefore, Canadas only attends shows to which he can drive, limiting him to a few per month.

*　*　*

Juel, located on a jewel of a street of unique homes, antique shops, art galleries, and cafes in Sydney, Australia, is a lovely jewelry shop. Two years old, the 50-square-meter shop is the second for partners Tegan Arnold and Elsa McMahon, who are also the two jewelry designers. Their original shop in a suburb of Sydney is seven years old and about 40 square meters. The superb displays and elegant décor of this shop are the finest anywhere in the world.

Juel's display window faces the street, but its entrance is on the courtyard side leading to other boutiques. A long, dramatically built showcase doubles for the window displays seen from the exterior as well as for interior displays. It is highlighted with two vases of tall fresh flowers on each end of the case, with the merchandise so originally featured that the effect is nothing short of dramatic. In fact, in a very understated way, a theatrical effect is the ambience of the entire shop.

The interior features tall, simple, elegant, three-sided glass cases, a neutral-tone upholstered couch and two chairs, and an elegant wood desk, the business center of the shop, placed unobtrusively in a back corner. Other than the lovely wood floors and startling spotlighting only of the jewelry, there is no other décor to detract from the drama of the merchandise or how it is displayed. Each décor piece counts.

The shop uses several items in an original manner for displays: tall, medium, and small vases; small cups; pieces of wood bark; and black-and-white flat ceramic tiles create a dramatic effect. Necklaces are draped around the necks of larger vases or laid on their sides with the necklaces across them. Earrings are hung on tiers of bark, on the rims of vases and cups, or stacked on tiles. Bracelets are "dripping" out of small vases. The shop uses vases to display coordinating pieces—necklaces hang down the front, bracelets hang on the neck, earrings hang on their rims. The display materials are incredibly effective, as are the displays themselves.

Highly polished wood floors, creative lighting, and elegant staging of merchandise at Juel.

The jewelry itself is beautiful, especially the collections that use various colors of semiprecious stones. Set mostly in silver but some gold, they appear in the tall showcases, one color per case. Each piece is displayed to its greatest advantage. The owner-designers have a staggering 29 different stones and six groups of colors from which to choose.

Groups of Colors:	*Kinds of Stones:*
1. Red, orange, pink, and coral	8
2. Blue, turquoise, and purple	6

3. Green and aquamarine   6
4. Pearl and shell   5
5. Black   2
6. Amber, brown, and yellow   2

Amazingly, there is a great range of prices. In Australian dollars, earrings range from $29 to $300; bracelets are $100–$700; and necklaces are $200 and up. Designs-to-order, of course, can run much higher.

On the subject of personnel, Tegan said:

> We look for different kinds of personalities but two main types are most prevalent: art students, in general, and actors. One of our star salespeople is impressive. She is a successful actress who works even when she has an acting job. She, like the others, is very responsible. You have to make your personnel feel they're part of a team, so you always strive for a relaxed and enjoyable atmosphere. They, in turn, must be relaxed, happy to be able to sell and to deal with difficult customers. And finally, they need to know that the owners are open to suggestions and are encouraged to give them.

Their most productive advertising is editorials, where magazine stylists borrow jewelry pieces for fashion shoots and write articles on what will be fashionable in the coming season. For special promotions they lend jewelry to society women for charity and music events. "We also donate pieces for charity auctions—many of them. In addition, we lend jewelry to TV presenters (anchors) to wear on the morning shows and on the evening news channels. We get a great deal of publicity for this." Additionally, they advertise in newspapers and magazines (especially wedding magazines).

Tegan and Elsa offered some secrets and tips for start-ups:

- ➤ Always stay in contact with the regular customer base—the people who put you in business and keep you in business.

- ➤ Never lose sight of what the average person wears (or does or thinks). Australia, for instance, is such a "casual dress" country that our jewelry must reflect that. It would be so easy to design stupendous pieces, but that's not Australia.

- ➤ Spend time locating the niche market for your business. To have, or be, a niche is the way to ensure you stay in business. In a country of small population, this is extraordinarily important. In fact, it is imperative.

Words that come to mind as I left Juel: *startling, dramatic, theatrical,* and just plain *lovely.*

* * *

This chapter in its own way is perhaps the second most important chapter in this book. Today, if you don't advertise, promote, and market your niche shop in at least one of the many ways suggested here, you may well find you are no longer in business.

Chapter 8

Bringing the Community Inside

Some of the shops I researched were just so good at public relations that I felt they deserved their own chapter. These are all shops that have found ways to incorporate promotions and special events into their everyday business life. They bring customers to them by creating activities inside the shop instead of having to pay for advertising. But it wasn't only their community spirit that stood out. They also fit all the other demanding criteria I used for my research, including great customer service; beautiful ambience, décor, and display; abundant inventory; and excellent location.

▶ Success Stories

Paul Fridlund bought his second-generation bookstore, ***Pilgrim's Way***, many years ago from his mother, who started the shop 40 years ago. People refer to the shop as an "alternative bookstore." Its inventory categories include sciences, astrology, Eastern and Western spirituality, environment, novels, biographies, new-age music and meditation CDs, prints, stationery, greeting cards, crystals, and items such as jewelry and scarves created by local craftspeople using natural materials.

Pilgrims Way, warm, harmonious, serene.

Together with his wife, Cynthia Fernandes, they operate a 700-square-foot shop, of which 600 is selling space. They also acquired the 850-square-foot "Secret Garden" behind Pilgrim's Way, which, as the name implies, carries a variety of succulents, ferns, seasonal vegetation, and garden accessories. The two areas are symbiotic, allowing bookshop customers to wander outdoors into the garden and read if they wish, or garden customers to wander inside and browse the books.

On the two occasions I visited the shop for interviews, I was quite surprised to observe that male customers outnumbered female customers four to one the first day and two to one a few days later. Both genders tended to make multiple purchases, especially the men.

Pilgrim's Way enjoys an ideal location close to the post office. As many locals walk by Pilgrim's Way as tourists, creating a 50/50 customer base. Every customer request and recommendation appears on the shelves as quickly as possible, stock is always kept current, and special orders are encouraged. Free gift wrapping is part of the shop's policy, and it offers a beautiful choice of papers, ribbons, and tissue.

Paul and Cynthia's marketing and special promotions have become a natural extension of their experience and inventory. Their goal has always been to have their bookshop considered "the hub of the community," and to that end they offer a huge five-by ten-foot in-store bulletin board devoted to brochures and promotions for local events (for customers and noncustomers alike). "Customers are drawn here because the ambience is so warm, harmonious, serene, and

On the way to the "Secret Garden."

spiritual, but not religious," explained Paul. In-store events are important to them, so a typical month includes a current events discussion group, a reading group, one or two new book signings, lectures, and discussions on any new subject suggested by customers or staff. "We're constantly putting people together for all sorts of reasons. We feel we're here to empower people." The concept works, because customers tell Paul and Cynthia that they leave the store feeling a bit better about themselves, which is exactly how these owners want their customers to feel. This is particularly true at a time when several book stores in their general area have gone out of business in the past few years. The staff is extremely important to Paul and Cynthia, who consider them part of their own family.

Paul and Cynthia attend several trade shows each year, such as those held by the American Booksellers Association and the Northern California Independent Booksellers Association. To collect new ideas and purchases for their garden shop, they attend the San Francisco International Gift Fair and the NOR CAL Spring Trade Show. For advertising, they do the following:

➤ Paul writes a book column in the local paper.

➤ They put a complimentary four-page monthly newsletter by the cash register.

➤ They promote the shop by talking about Pilgrim's Way to people in inns, hotels, and other shops, often going door to door.

Here is some of their advice to new start-ups:

➤ You must be different and individual, like no other shop of your kind—a true niche business.

➤ You must reflect what you love doing.

➤ You must have excellent, personal service.

* * *

Normally, I would not include the following shop in this book because at the time I was there it had just celebrated its one-year anniversary. But I am so sure that this happy shop will be a success for years to come that I decided to use it as an example of a shop that has all the right ingredients and is my best bet to succeed.

Bella and Daisy's is part of the Union Street Shops and the Fillmore Street Shops complexes located in a trendy shopping area of San Francisco. The complexes are perpendicular to each other. The first is five blocks long, and the second is about eight blocks long. Both are composed of shops and cafés that are funky, chic, inexpensive, and expensive. The most outstanding shop in the entire area, however, is Bella and Daisy's. Melissa Louis, the owner, emphatically told me that the location is "absolutely ideal."

Bella and Daisy's is a dog bakery and boutique. It stands out for several reasons. One is the approach to the white front door. The first thing one sees is a white picket fence surrounding a grassy gardenlike area that hosts some delightful recycled metal sculptures, a dog house, a hydrant sculpture, a dog bowl, and a bone. Down three brick steps is a brick terrace furnished with a white garden table and chairs and a row of dog carriages (the latter are

Bella and Daisy's clientele pause for a snapshot.

167

for sale, as are the items in the grass area). Finally there is the door itself, the lower half of which is a white picket gate enclosing the dogs within. It creates a quaint Dutch-door effect. Peering in, I saw what looked like a very charming children's shop, so abundant was the merchandise and the manner in which it was all displayed. The approximately 1,800-square-foot space was open and airy, yet cozy, with several large windows and soft lighting.

At the time I was there, the shop was ably staffed by one dedicated full-time employee and one fill-in employee.

Specialty food and treats are up front, including bakery goods such as doggy pastries, cupcakes, cannolis, cookies of all sorts, bread bones, and birthday party cakes—all made with doggy ingredients, of course, and all displayed in a bakery case. Specialty canned foods are displayed in a white bookcase. Five tables (all of the display furniture are antique and timeless pieces that Melissa picked up at garage sales, secondhand shops, and the like) down the center of the shop hold clothing, including shirts, tank tops, and sweaters. Next to these are the homeopathics—vitamins, remedies, shampoos, and coat scents, all displayed on white bookcases. A small cat corner offers kitty treats, toys, books, totes, frames, and cat bowls.

On the opposite side of the door is a cozy lounge area—a corner, really—consisting of a homey couch, chairs, and coffee table, strewn with dog throws and pillows, that doubles as a "living room" for the staff members to sit and chat with their friends. All customers become their friends while the "children" (read: dogs) cavort freely around the shop. Antique and modern dog prints hang on the wall above the couch. A huge, gorgeous fresh-flower arrangement (changed every week) on a ledge behind the couch lends further warmth to the bright and cheerful ambience. And to act as a divider next to the "humans" area is another old bookcase, painted white and containing organic and vegetarian treats.

An 18-foot wall space is hung with collars and leashes of all types, from basic to rhinestones and sparkles, ranging in price from $13 to $140, including a San Francisco designer's line. Above that are dog bags selling for $300 to $500. Large cubby-holed bookcases contain pet carriers ($84–$520) and beds of all sorts ($40-$100). Some small cubbyholes hold toys and bowls and others hold treat jars. Finally, there are racks of hanging coats and sweaters along the wall; above them hang rhinestone necklaces, charms, and other baubles.

The back room is used for all the bagged, canned, and raw foods because, of course, there is no eye appeal to them.

The square footage is large for such an enterprise—I've never seen larger—and very cleverly Melissa offsets the rental expense by subletting two offices in the extra space beyond the food section in the back of the shop. This is very clever—not only because the income makes the rent affordable but also because the two renters have dogs themselves, and one of them doubles as the part-time salesperson and does other kinds of chores.

Two of Melissa's staff members hastened to say that they are not considered "employees" as such but rather that they are part of a team—the first tenet of the shop's philosophy. The overall philosophy, she continued, "is to promote services and items of neighborhood businesses" such as artists' and photographers' works pertaining to dogs. Their portraits and framed photographs hang on the walls (each of these creative contributors accept commissions as well).

Everything Bella and Daisy's does is geared to the neighborhood, where I observed that almost every other person owns at least one dog. In fact, the team considers itself "the hub of the neighborhood" because it is so involved with its neighbors—young and old, rich and poor, females and males alike. Right from the beginning, for instance, the shop donated a gift basket of goodies (worth over $200) to as many of the local charities as requested them. It still does. A very clever event every Friday is "Yappie Hour" from 4:00 to 6:00 p.m., where owners are served wine and cheese and their dogs are given treats. Both the humans and the dogs meet old and new friends. Bella and Daisy's offered gift wrapping from the first day of opening. On their first anniversary, an announcement was sent out that read in part:

> *Please join us for an elegant evening in celebration of our one-year anniversary. To thank our wonderful community, we are hosting a silent auction to benefit Galileo High School.*

Intended or not, this is a great way to make older students (present and future pet owners) aware of Bella and Daisy's.

For the first six months she was in business, Melissa hired a public relations person who came up with an ad package for local magazines, newspapers, radio stations, and TV stations. One ad appeared on the local morning news program on which Melissa once also had an interview. It generated so much interest in the shop that at the end of the six-month contract, Melissa cancelled all formal advertising. Word-of-mouth was sufficient from then on, along with the various events and promotions the staff itself was planning.

Bella and Daisy's has two websites: one is a co-op site with other shops on Union Street, maintained by sfbayshop.com. It includes Bella and Daisy's in its wonderful promotional site for participating shops. The second is the shop's own site (bellaanddaisys .com), which is an interactive e-commerce site selling their niche products online. Internet shoppers can e-mail the store, order products, and receive a free newsletter through this site, which is more personal than the co-op site.

Not only is Bella and Daisy's becoming well-known to human customers, but even an occasional dog finds its way to the shop for a little help. There have been occasions where lost dogs turned up at the shop and one of the team has recognized it and called the "parents" to come pick it up. When a customer was sick recently, each of the team contributed to a dinner for her and delivered it to her home. Another customer, who came to the shop to ask for a recommendation for a kennel to board her dog while she was away, was astonished when a staff member said, "Are you kidding? I'll take her while you're away!" That customer is now one of the store's best customers and friends.

Here are two more of Bella and Daisy's business secrets:

➤ Customers become friends, and as such there is a personal relationship among the dog owners, the dogs, and us.

➤ We treat Bella and Daisy's not as a business but as our home, where our customer friends come to visit us.*

* * *

Since I interviewed May Waldroup about **Thunderbird Bookshop**, she retired after over 40 years of owning and operating that business. But what Waldroup accomplished at Thunderbird and throughout the community is such a positive example of retailing success that it is still a marvelous example for new niche shop owners.

After two early moves, Thunderbird Bookshop settled in a loca-

*Just prior to publication of this book, Frank O'Daniel became a co-owner of Bella and Daisy's.

tion that May Waldroup and her husband built in a quaint shopping center in Carmel, California. Since they built their building, the rest of the shopping center has grown up around them.

From the beginning, Thunderbird was never just another bookstore; it was a good-sized shop with a large café and reading room. There were two parts to the café: one inside with a fireplace; the other an enclosed porch with a retractable roof. Both served as special-event venues. May explained that it was the first such combination in the country, as far as she knows. Because the Monterey area is home to many published writers, May had a special section of her shop just for books written by local authors.

Events, she explained, encompassed all of the following and more:

> Art shows and artist receptions

> Poetry readings

> Travel slide shows

> Lectures by national and local authors, experts in particular categories

> Charity fundraisers

> Musical events

> Garden events

➤ Dinners

➤ Book signings

There was even a wedding in the store for two book lovers who specifically loved Thunderbird, and May hosted a reception for them.

For many years May had an entire area devoted to metaphysics, which was extremely popular with locals and tourists. It stocked books, crystals, tarot cards, incense, fragrant candles, gifts, and the like. Local card readers or psychics could leave their brochures and flyers in a handy display case, free to the public.

"It was," said May, "really a little cultural center catering to all interests." Indeed, through the years the shop became a meeting center for book lovers, discussion groups, and would-be authors.

May is a recognizable authority on books of all categories, and her recommendations were a hallowed tradition. Every repeat customer, upon entering the shop, first checked the long table at the front of the shop where May displayed her reading suggestions, and there were many—ranging from the latest bestsellers, to classics, to poetry, to history, to science. In four decades nobody has disliked a book from that collection, as far as anyone knew. Her shop also stocked magazines, gift cards, small gifts, newspapers, and audio books.

May insisted on book-loving, literate staff members who had good memories, technical skills, and could act as advisors. She added that she insisted they possess the following people skills:

➤ Know that the customer is always right.

➤ "Kill them with kindness" when one is dealing with unhappy customers.

Thunderbird also provided gift certificates, gift wrapping, a good return policy, and many other customer delights. Many of the staff members were with her for years.

Always interested in people, May has been active in community affairs for decades. Here is some of her advice to potential bookshop owners:

➤ Become involved as soon as possible in the community.

➤ A shop can be a stage for all types of events, charities, cultural groups, and individuals. You are in a unique position to hold such events.

➤ Due to the enormous changes in the book business, *don't* go into the new book business; rather, start a secondhand used book shop. That's where you want to be today.

➤ Create a website right from the get-go.

Not every bookstore can install a café on its premises, although May advises having one if you can. The combination of sitting comfortably and quietly in a cozy ambience with a cup of coffee, next to a fireplace, while browsing books is a book lover's heaven. And that was May's goal.

*   *   *

This chapter highlights the theme that runs throughout the book: Involvement. Be involved. Stay involved. Whether it's with individuals who are customers or with the community—especially the neighborhood community—your involvement is essential to success. The reason: It connects you to potential customers who will help you become successful!

Chapter 9

Your Grand Opening

Making your Grand Opening sizzle—an event to remember—requires preliminary planning and effort on your part, which includes becoming involved with your community or neighborhood in a voluntary capacity. As soon as you have decided on the location of your shop, take the time to join (preferably to become a committee member of) a nonprofit civic, charitable, or business group. Libraries, museums, historic societies, welcoming committees, aquariums, botanical gardens, sports centers, theater and music societies, business associations, chambers of commerce, and charity organizations all offer excellent contacts, depending on your niche category.

If your niche is related to art, becoming a committee member of a local art museum or art association will get you known to people who can send you business. And just as important, you will get to know the type of people you *want* as customers. If your specialty is related to animals, a natural tie-in would be the Society for the Prevention of Cruelty to Animals (SPCA) or animal shelters in your area. If your niche is children, a natural charity is a children's hospital, children's cancer ward, or groups that care for needy children. Your involvement not only benefits your business, it would be time well spent for a worthy cause.

Whatever organization you choose, as you build your business and your charitable contacts, your name will become known in the community in positive terms. Often the local papers cover the special events at these nonprofit groups, so there is the added benefit of having your photo in newspapers or appearing as a guest on local TV or radio as a constructive member of your community. From all of your personal and business contacts you will build a sizeable invitation list for your Grand Opening.

You can add to that list by checking various sections of your newspaper for those who have a connection to your specialty. Check the social, business, literary, drama, lifestyle, and business sections of the paper. (Most newspaper articles are now also online.) If your shop is animal related, send invitations to all the veterinary offices in your town; if it's bridal related, send invitations to all the wedding coordinators at churches in your area, all the wedding consulting companies, and all the wedding caterers in your area. Whatever your specialty, brainstorm as many ways to find related contacts as you possibly can for invitation purposes. You can get street addresses and e-mail addresses from the online yellow pages.

Invitations

Because you might not have e-mail addresses for some people or street addresses for others, you will probably use a mix of e-mail and mail. It's also a good idea, if you have time, to personally call VIP guests.

The least expensive way to create invitations is by designing them yourself on your computer. Depending on how sophisticated you are with design, you can create a beautiful yet simple invitation and send it as an attachment to your e-mail. The recipient can print the attached invitation and save it as a reminder. If you cannot create graphics, a written e-mail invitation will work well. Be sure to include the who, what, where, when, and why:

➤ Your name and the name of the shop.

➤ What type of event it is (Grand Opening), and the type of entertainment that is included.

➤ The address, day, date, and time.

➤ The nonprofit group that will benefit from the event and what, if anything, is expected, such as canned goods for a "feed the needy" charity; wrapped toys for a children's charity; a small donation for a museum charity, etc.

You can also choose from an assortment of predesigned, ready-to-mail invitation cards from catalogs. If you plan to send out attractive mailers on a regular basis, which you should, choosing from supply catalogs makes things very easy. No matter what your specialty, there are industry supply catalogs available through the Internet. You can find them by searching for "business promotional supplies" or "stationery and paper supplies."

If your budget allows, you can order custom-designed invitations from a local printer, including matching envelopes.

Displays

Gussy up everything in the shop to make it appear exciting—windows, doors, interior and exterior displays, and clever displays of all your merchandise.

Entertainment

Local musicians who play regularly at weddings will often agree to perform free at your Grand Opening in exchange for some free publicity in your shop. You could arrange to put their poster, business cards, or flyers in your shop for a month. Exchanging services can be very beneficial in business. Both sides get something they need from the exchange.

Entertainment should be kept simple. Good ideas include a guitarist, caricaturist, fortune teller, ventriloquist, clown, stilt walker, children's musician, a face painter (for children or adults), a mime, or a one- or two-person puppet show.

A health- or exercise-related shop might hire a young gymnast—who can work in a small space—to put on a special performance.

An international-food shop could hire an Irish dancer or a fiddler.

If your charity is the Salvation Army, for example, you may be lucky enough to secure a few members of its band, which will entertain and unobtrusively collect money outside.

If your niche is related to the military and you have a military base nearby, contact the base's public relations officer and ask if they have a small choir that would sing a few patriotic songs to get your opening off to a rousing start. Most military choirs offer this service to the community free of charge and are delighted to perform—and they wear full dress uniform.

Giveaways

Another way to get free help is to ask your vendors/suppliers what they could contribute to your grand opening. Many times they will want to be involved with your events from the very beginning and offer "freebies" for your guests. Some might even offer to underwrite some of the cost of the event, depending on what you can offer them in exchange.

Your giveaways/mementos should be useful items that are related to your specialty, if possible. Whatever they are, be sure your logo is printed on them. Here are some good giveaway items:

➤ A bride-and-groom key chain (good for bridal shop openings)

➤ A small flashlight (good for hardware shops)

➤ A bib (good for infants' or children's shops)

➤ A pot holder (good for kitchen supply shops)

➤ A tennis ball, golf ball, headband, or sun visor (good for a sports or exercise shop)

You can find hundreds of ideas for giveaways in catalogs, under the "business promotional items" category. All items can be imprinted with your logo.

Prizes

Raffles are always popular. An easy way to hold a raffle is to place as many of your guests' business cards or names and addresses as you can into a beautiful bowl or jar. Then, simply have one of the guests pick one out toward the end of your grand opening. The person whose name is on the card wins the prize.

Another, and more creative, way to give prizes—and at the same time increase your future business—is to fill a bowl with small pieces of paper (discount coupons). Some pieces of paper read "10 percent off," others will say "20 percent off," and yet others will say "30 percent off." All should offer at least 5 percent off. Each customer can then return to the store and purchase an item using the discount coupon.

If your merchandise is expensive, such as wedding gowns in a bridal shop, the discount coupons could read in dollars rather than percentages, such as "$25 off," "$50 off," or "$100 off."

You can set a time limit on the use of the discounts by writing an expiration date on the coupons. Write in a date that is a least 30 days away, but try not to go longer than a year, so that you won't have to keep honoring them five years later! For some categories, such as bridal gowns, your single or engaged-to-be-married guests might not be ready to use the discounts for a year or more. But chances are, if they have a discount offer, they will return to your shop when they are ready.

Naturally, not all the guests will use the coupons, but it is an excellent goodwill promotion for future business, and your guests will feel as if you have indeed rewarded them for attending your grand opening.

It is *important* to make clear that the cash amount of any discounts will be given to the nonprofit beneficiary of the event.

Refreshments

The least expensive menu would be foods that you or your friends can prepare: a vegetable platter with a couple of dips, bite-size cheese cubes, bite-size cookies (to reduce the crumb factor), and punch. A midprice offering might include all of the above, plus finger sandwiches or rolls with cream cheese, chopped black or green olives, or herb mixture and tomato slices. A more substantial choice would be to add meat or deli platters. You can purchase a wide variety of ready-made hors d'oeuvres platters at your local supermarket or deli.

If you have a large budget, consider having your grand opening catered.

If your shop is food or cooking related, a local deli or catering company might welcome the opportunity to provide you with free samples of its goods for your guests, in exchange for you handing out its business cards.

Whatever you serve, remember that you have a shop full of expensive merchandise, so be sure to provide napkins or towelettes for guests to wipe their hands.

Soft drinks, coffee, tea, or a punch should be available, depending on the time of day. Champagne punch is fitting for a Grand Opening, as long as zoning laws don't forbid alcohol on the premises.

Instead of plain paper plates and napkins, choose colorful paper goods. It spiffs up the event and the presentation of the food.

Guest Book

The most important tool you can use for adding to your contact list is to have a guest book in a prominent place and ask people to sign it. It should have space for an address, e-mail, home or business phone, cell phone, and comments. Although not everyone will provide personal information, those who do are obviously interested in hearing from you and will make excellent contacts for your future events and sales.

Promoting the Grand Opening

As I mentioned in Chapter 7, e-mail or mail a press release to the media, either to the news desk or individual reporters at your local media outlets, or present yourself in person and make a personal contact.

Bear in mind that media today—whether it is print, TV, or radio—is terribly understaffed, and usually receives several hundred, if not thousands, of press releases every week from around their towns, cities, states, and the country. So unless your Grand Opening is truly special, don't expect that the media will automatically use your news. It usually takes something special to get the media interested in a new shop opening.

For example, an art gallery owner in Monterey, California, hired an artistic elephant to paint original pictures outside his gallery for an hour. Accompanied by a trainer, the elephant picked up the paintbrush with her trunk, chose her own paint colors, and painted whatever she felt like painting on each piece of art paper. The paintings were then auctioned off for charity. That was so unusual that a TV station sent out a cameraman to capture the event for the local evening news.

A shopping center that was promoting its Grand Opening with a benefit for the Society for the Prevention of Cruelty to Animals

(SPCA) invited a famous actress who is well-known for her love of animals. She cut the red ribbon at the entrance to the center. The involvement of a celebrity or VIP is the type of event guaranteed to attract media coverage.

If you have a website, devote a page to your grand-opening information weeks in advance.

Remember always that you are a specialty business, so no matter what your niche category might be, promote it in a clever, unique, and even off-beat way if you want to get attention.

A Bridal Shop Opening

A Grand Opening should be exactly that: grand! I am including an example of a *Grand* Opening I witnessed for a bridal shop in New Jersey, and of course all the ideas that were used in this case can be adapted to other niche categories.

The first thing the guests saw when they arrived was a white stretch limousine parked in front of the shop. Attached to the roof were a large Raggedy Anne and Andy dressed in bridal garb, surrounded by lots of balloons—some flying high, others attached to the front and rear of the limo. A very large sign read: "Just Married To . . ." and the name of the shop followed. From the interior of the limo came the strains of taped wedding music. (If you plan to use a limo or other vehicle parked on the street, special permission may be required, depending on your zoning regulations.) A red carpet led from the limo to the front door of the shop.

Inside the shop were eight models: two wore wedding gowns, five wore bridesmaid's dresses, and one wore a flower girl dress. They were all friends of the owner; some were engaged to be married, and all were potential future customers of the shop. They took turns walking around the shop, standing near the front door welcoming guests, or standing in the display window for a short time. The flower girl scattered white blossoms from a basket into the windows and down the red carpet (confetti could also be used).

Each of the models invited an average of three friends and suggested they also invite their friends. That gave the owner a potential customer list of over two dozen, just from these ladies and their friends, without any advertising expense!

At this particular Grand Opening, the music inside the shop was a trio that played regularly at weddings in the area.

A lovely addition to the refreshment menu was a small piece of wedding cake for each guest. (If you plan on owning a bridal shop, check with bakeries in your area to see if they would like to provide free cake samples.)

The shop owner filled the guest book with contacts, and the Grand Opening got the business off to a great start. With that type of creativity, the owners undoubtedly did a splendid job of promoting their shop.

A Shocking Display

In the 1970s we had a bridal salon in our department store, and just prior to its opening I took a course in window dressing from the foremost window designer in the country. He had designed the very first "naughty" magazine ad in the U.S. and taught us to design windows that *shock*. (In the '70s, window displays were becoming more "experimental and daring" than in previous decades.)

So I designed the four front windows. Each window portrayed

a gorgeously clad wedding party in beautiful settings. In the fourth window was the bride, alone. With a naked light bulb overhead, the mannequin was seen wearing a lovely long veil—that the buyer had ordered specially handmade for this window—a pair of white satin heels, and only a white ribbon draped across her front, from left shoulder to right hip. When we unveiled the windows the morning of the opening, it became *an event*—a shock to some in that conservative town, but a "happening" for others. It was a smash hit! Our bridal salon became the "in" place to shop for the entire wedding party.

* * *

If you take the suggestions here and expand on them with your own creativity, your Grand Opening will be one to remember!

* * *

In conclusion, if you remember just a few basic rules, including the most important in all of retailing—the Right Item, at the Right Price, in the Right Place, at the Right Time—you will almost guarantee your success in business as one of the 15 percent of shops that survive and prosper.

However many or few niche categories you create, be sure to keep your specialty shop image and reputation intact. Build a strong business office foundation. Create a unique enterprise with ingenuity and originality.

Good luck! And don't forget to enjoy yourself, to have fun as you give life to your new enterprise!

Trade and Gift Shows

Trade and Gift Shows

Below is a list of some of the most prominent trade shows in the U.S. and Canada. Some trade shows are annual, but some are semi-annual. I've noted the show venues as well as the major categories each show caters to.

January

➤ **California Gift Show**—Los Angeles Convention Center—and California Market Center Gift & Home Market—California Market Center—includes home furnishings, scents (called extracts), fashion, accessories, jewelry (called cash and carry), kids, outdoor, stationery, tabletop, and housewares

➤ **New York International Gift Fair**—Jacob Javits Convention Center—includes general giftware, tabletop and housewares, decorative and personal accessories, personal care and wellness products, museum gifts, ethnic, traditional, country and contemporary crafts, specialty foods, contemporary design products, juvenile products, floral and outdoor living products, and pet products

➤ **Orlando Gift Show**—Orange County Convention Center

➤ **Atlanta Gift Fair**—Georgia World Congress Center—includes American country, home decor, garden and floral accents, general tabletop, and housewares

➤ **Dallas International Gift and Home Accessories Market**—Dallas Market Center—includes home decor; garden and floral accents; general gift; handmade; kids; mind, body, and spirit; personal style; and jewelry

➤ **Toronto International Gift Fair**—Metro Toronto Convention Center—includes: home decor, body and soul, handmade, garden and floral accessories, general giftware, personal style, and specialty foods

➤ **The Seattle Gift Show**—Washington State Convention and Trade Center—includes handmade and personal style

➤ **Washington, D.C. Gift Show**—Washington Convention Center—includes at home, floral and garden accessories, general gifts and handmade

February

➤ **San Francisco International Gift Fair**—The Moscone Center—includes accent on design, at home, handmade, kids, and the museum source

➤ **East Coast Show (New Brunswick, Canada)**—Moncton Coliseum Complex

➤ **Alberta Gift Show (Edmonton, Canada)**—Northlands Agricom, Edmonton

March

➤ **New York Home Textiles Show (NYHTS)**—Metropolitan Pavilion—includes bed, bath, dining, linens, windows, floor, and home accessories, 500 exhibitors

➤ **New York Extracts Show**—Metropolitan Pavilion—includes aromatherapy, fragrance and personal care, 300 exhibitors

➤ **New York Cash & Carry . . . Gifts to Go Show**—Jacob Javits Convention Center—includes general giftware, tabletop and housewares, decorative and personal accessories, museum gifts, ethnic, traditional, contemporary crafts, contemporary design products, floral products, and jewelry

➤ **Los Angeles Fashion, Gift & Home Market**—California Market Center

➤ **Boston Gift Show—Boston Convention & Exhibition Center**—includes at home, general gifts, handmade, made in New England, souvenirs, and the museum source

➤ **Dallas International Gift & Home Accessories Market**—Dallas Market Center—includes general gift and jewelry

➤ **Montreal Gift Show—Place Bonaventure**—apparel, fashion accessories, contemporary handcrafted, general gift, gourmet food, garden accessories, holiday/floral, home and décor, housewares, jewelry, stationery, tourist/resort

➤ **Vancouver Gift Show**—BC Place Stadium

May

➤ **San Francisco Gourmet Products Show**—The Moscone Center

➤ **New York International Contemporary Furniture Fair**—Jacob Javits Convention Center

➤ **National Stationery Show, New York**—Jacob Javits Convention Center

June

➤ **Dallas International Gift & Home Accessories Market**—Dallas Market Center (same as January)

July

➤ **Atlanta Gift Fair**—Georgia World Congress Center (same as January)

➤ **Los Angeles Gift & Home Market and California Gift Show**—California Market Center (same as January)

➤ **San Francisco International Gift Fair**—The Moscone Center (same as February)

➤ **Washington, D.C. Gift Show**—Washington Convention Center (same as January)

August

➤ **New York International Gift Fair**—Jacob Javits Convention Center (same as January)

➤ **Orlando Gift Show**—Orange County Convention Center (same as January)

➤ **The Seattle Gift Show**—Washington State Convention and Trade Center (same as January)

➤ **Alberta Gift Show**—Northlands Agricom (same as February)

➤ **Montreal Gift Show**—Place Bonaventure (same as March)

September

➤ **Boston Gift Show**—Boston Convention & Exhibition Center (same as March)

➤ **Los Angeles Gift and Home Market Show**—California Market Center (same as July)

➤ **Dallas International Gift & Home Accessories Market**—Dallas Market Center (same as June)

October

➤ **New York Home Textiles Show**—Jacob Javits Convention Center—presented as part of House to Home Market Week and Extracts Show

Apparel Trade Shows

Womenswear

CITY	VENUE	MONTH
ATLANTA	Atlanta Market Center	May
ATLANTA	Atlanta Apparel Mart	April, October
ATLANTA	Atlanta Southern Bridal Show (unknown venue)	August

CHICAGO	Chicago National Bridal Market Chicago Apparel Center	March, October
DALLAS	Women's Summer Apparel Market Dallas Market Center	January
DALLAS	Dallas Bridal Show Dallas Market Center	August, March, October
LAS VEGAS	Las Vegas International Lingerie Show "The largest lingerie show in the U.S." (no venue given)	April
LAS VEGAS	WWD Magic International Show "The world's largest and most important women's apparel exhibition covers every area of women's and juniors" Las Vegas Convention Center	February, August
LOS ANGELES	LA Fall Market Week California Mart	April
LOS ANGELES	LA Fall/Holiday Market Week California Mart	June
LOS ANGELES	LA Fashions Week "California Designers Only" California Market Center	March, June, August, October

LOS ANGELES	LA Holiday/Resort Market Week California Market Center	August
LOS ANGELES	Junior & Contemporary Market California Market Center	April, October
LOS ANGELES	LA Shoe Show California Mart	January, April, June, August, November
LOS ANGELES	LA Spring Market Week California Market Center	October
LOS ANGELES	LA Summer Market Week California Mart	January
LOS ANGELES	Pacific Champions Sportswear Show LA Convention Center	April
MARLBOROUGH, MASSACHUSETTS (BOSTON)	New England Apparel Club New England Apparel Market	January, April, June, October
NEW YORK	Lingerie—American Show of Intimate Apparel & Lingerie Metropolitan Pavilion	February
SAN FRANCISCO	San Francisco Children's Apparel Market Concourse Exhibition Center	April, June

Menswear

CITY	VENUE	MONTH
ATLANTA	Atlanta Apparel Mart	February, April, June, October
CHICAGO	Chicago Apparel Center	February
CHICAGO	Market Week Chicago Apparel Center	February, August

Mens Specialty Shops

CITY	VENUE	MONTH
DALLAS	The Men's Show Dallas Market Center	February, August, October
LAS VEGAS	Magic Show "Largest men's apparel trade show in the world" Las Vegas Convention Center	February, August
LOS ANGELES	The Urban Suburban Streetwear Show "For young men & juniors" California Market Center	March, October
MIAMI	Big & Tall Show Radisson Hotel	February

194

| NEW YORK | Big & Tall Show Radisson Hotel | February |

Childrenswear

CITY	VENUE	MONTH
LAS VEGAS	Magic Kids "Largest children's (boys and girls) show in the U.S." Las Vegas Convention Center	February, August
NEW YORK	American International Clothing and Toys Fair	February
SAN FRANCISCO	San Francisco Children's Apparel Market	April, June

Men's & Boy's

CITY	VENUE	MONTH
DALLAS	Men's & Boys' Apparel Market Dallas Market Center	January, March, October
HONOLULU	Men's and Women's Hawaii Market Merchandise Expo	January, April, September, November
LAS VEGAS	Men's and Women's Las Vegas Convention Center	June
MIAMI	Men's & Boys' Apparel Show (no venue given)	January

ORLANDO, FLORIDA	Fine Jewelry Show Orange County Convention Center	January
ORLANDO, FLORIDA	PGA Merchandise Show Men's and Women's Golfware Orange County Convention Center	January
SAN FRANCISCO	San Francisco Men's and Women's Fashion Weeks Concourse Exhibition Center	January, April, June
SEATTLE	Seattle Trend Show for Men and Women Seahawks Exhibition Center	January, April, June

Men's, Women's, and Children's

CITY	VENUE	MONTH
DALLAS	Men's, Women's and Children's Swimwear Dallas Market Center	August, October
DALLAS	Men's, Women's and Children's Regional Western Apparel Market "for TOLA Retailers—offered by Western Manufacturers"	January
LAS VEGAS	World Shoe Association Show	February, August

Sands Expo & Convention
Center
"The largest footwear show
in the U.S."

CITY	VENUE	MONTH
MIAMI	Miami Swim Show "The largest swimwear tradeshow in the world" Miami International Merchandise Mart	February, July
MIAMI	Shoe Market of the Americas "Showcases the entire spectrum of all footwear companies" Miami Radisson Center	March, June
NEW YORK	New York Jewelry Market JA New York Summer Show Jacob Javits Convention Center	January, July
NEW YORK	New York Accessories Market	January, March, April, August, November
NEW YORK	New York Shoe Expo "Largest shoe show on the U.S. East Coast"	June, December

Women's and Children's

CITY	VENUE	MONTH
ATLANTA	Women's & Children's Wear Atlanta Apparel Mart	January, June

CHICAGO	Chicago Apparel Market	January, June
	Chicago Apparel Center	
DALLAS	Dallas Apparel Mart	May, August
	Dallas Market Center	
	Women's, Children's, and	
	Accessories	
SAN FRANCISCO	San Francisco Women's and	January,
	Children's Market	October
	Concourse Exhibition Center	

Other Types of Shows

CITY	VENUE	MONTH
NEW YORK	National Stationery Show Jacob Javits Convention Center	May

Buying Offices

In addition to trade shows, there are also buying offices, which are trade organizations to which you receive membership for a yearly fee, for the purpose of getting help with the buying as well as making the job simpler and easier. A buying office buyer of childrenswear, for instance, may present at a seasonal show—or perhaps individually—20 items just for infants. She is an infants buyer who may have had some of the items manufactured just for her and her buying office in several foreign countries. Or she may have made the same sorts of deals with her favorite small manufacturers here in this country for just one or two items from each one. Instead of a shop owner running around to 10 different manufacturers' showrooms, which is extremely time-consuming two or three times a year, the retailer can see several of the same 20 items that, bought in bulk for the clients of the buying office, will be cheaper for the retailer. The items might be manufactured especially for the infants buyer, which means the items are original items exclusively for clients of the buying office.

To save time and money, then, it is often of great advantage for retailers to belong to a buying office. The value lies in the fact that in one place you can view the trends, view the most important items of a whole category, get advice, and have private consultations about the direction of your own shop. And that certainly is advisable. I know that we couldn't have been as successful as we were without the help of resident buyers, especially in the children's, juniors', and contemporary markets. In fact, in the juniors' and contemporary categories, where fashion trends change so rapidly, the help the buying office provides is invaluable. They also offer "programs" of imports—that is, items manufactured in other countries exclusively for a buying office. This enables a small retailer to take advantage of "special" prices that generate greater profits; sometimes much greater profits.

Another advantage of certain buying offices is that they offer "off price" (a sale of wholesale merchandise) goods exclusively for greater profitability. And in this era of fierce competition in the retail arena, it is imperative that you stay alert and sharp vis-à-vis your judgments and choices.

Of course, the services of a buying office do not come free. The fees can be somewhat steep for a business in its first few years of operation. But often the ultimate profits, after buying office fees, can make it very worthwhile. It may be a matter of squeezing the cost out of your budget—a kind of robbing Peter to pay Paul—to find the funds for such an extra necessity. In any case, you have nothing to lose by looking into it.

You may be surprised that there are many different methods of payment for buying office services depending upon your requirements. One office may charge a fee for a particular service but the next might be cheaper and include a second service. So it is in your best interests to look into as many buying offices as possible. They can and usually do, in the end, add to your profits.

Perhaps because most apparel used to be manufactured in New York City, most buying offices, likewise, are in New York. Over the years, however, a few have sprung up in other places. Los Angeles, for instance, manufactured certain types of apparel, so buying offices sprang up in that city and in other large cities for similar reasons.

The list of buying offices presented here is not a complete list by any means—especially outside New York—but it will give you an idea of where to begin. In addition, I have underlined any unique categories a resource has. Also, I have categorized the offices by city, by group, and by sizes. The men's group is designated with an M; the women's with W; children's with C; and juniors' with Jrs. Accessories are indicated by an A, and boys and girls by B and G. You can also research buying offices on the Internet.

New York City

BUYING OFFICE	CATEGORIES AND SIZES
1. Actis Grande Assoc. 1333 Broadway Phone: 212-759-6111	Accessories

2. Barbara Fields Buying Office
   110 East Ninth St.
   Phone: 212-627-6474

   Jrs., W, A—moderate to better—*"full service fashion consultants in the juniors' market"* Los Angeles & New York offices—specialty stores

3. Barzilay Goldberg Buying Office
   450 Seventh Ave.
   Phone: 212-244-6147

4. Beverly's Best Buys
   240 West 35th St.
   Phone: 212-563-5234

   M, B, G—"a hands-on B.O. specializing in the above"

5. Big Lots Buying Office
   1270 Broadway
   Phone: 212-868-1950

   M, W, C, and A—*off price*

6. Butler Buying Service
   11 Riverside Dr.
   Phone: 212-724-6350

   W—sportswear, dresses, suits, outerwear

7. Carol Hoffman Buying Office
   110 West 40th St.
   Phone: 212-382-3805

   W—misses, petites, plus sizes "*a high end specialty store co.* dedicated to promoting greater profitability . . . *full market assistance* or *consultation levels of service*"

8. Custom Buying Service
   566 Seventh Ave.
   Phone: 212-391-5699

   W—moderate-to-better RTW "some specialty stores"

9. Denise Minsky Buying Group
   65 West 36th St.
   Phone: 212-695-8383

   M, W, C—"Budget to Moderate"

10. Dianne Cohan Assoc.
    1412 Broadway
    Phone: 212-719-3008

    W, G, Jrs.—misses, petite and large sizes, *leather apparel & sporting goods, "personalized one-on-one services, multiunit specialty stores"*

11. Dis Outfitters
    44 West 55th St.
    Phone: 212-399-0750

    M, W (misses) apparel and A—"Better specialty stores"

12. Excelsior Fashion Inc.
    1407 Broadway
    Phone: 212-575-1740

    M, W, C, A—regular and off price—also: *footwear*—petite and plus sizes

13. Fashion Connection Buying Office
    110 West 40th St.
    Phone: 212-947-5005

    M, C, Jrs.—misses, plus sizes, "with personalized service"

14. Fashion Express
    240 West 35th St.
    Phone: 212-244-1409

    W, A—moderate, better; contemporary, bridge

15. Gabe Mozarsky Co.
    150 West 30th
    Phone: 212-465-8030

    M, W—*leather apparel, furs,* outerwear

16. Gregor Simmons
    224 West 35th St.
    Phone: 212-643-9590

    W, A—*contemporary,* jrs., misses petite, plus sizes—better *young designers*

17. Herbert J. Gluckson Buying Service
    330 East 49th St.
    Phone: 212-921-4250

    W—jrs., misses, W sizes, "*specialty shops,* moderate and off price . . . *guidance and consultations*"; also M—"off price specialist" in *men's and plus sizes*

18. Jane Tucker Enterprises
    320 Central Park West
    Phone: 212-496-4046
    Fax: 212-877-0260

    Designer and couture—dresses, sportswear, gowns, skirts, outerwear, accessories

19. Joanne Evans
    450 Seventh Ave.
    Phone: 212-643-3636

    W—better to contemporary—sportswear, dresses, outerwear, *millinery*—for jrs., petites, large and plus sizes.

20. J. W. Merchandising
    80 N. Moore St.
    Phone: 212-285-2024

    W—"a resident buying office to assist *specialty stores* . . . for the *luxury* market . . . covers the market, edits lines, reports on trends . . ."

21. Lady Budd Affiliates Lba Buying
    501 Seventh Ave.
    Phone: 212-768-8231

    W, A—moderate to better sportswear, dresses, "*innovative buying service with professional guidance . . . to increase profitability* for *independently-owned specialty stores serving their local communities*"

22. *Martin Bayer Assoc.*
    171 West 57th St.
    Phone: 212-586-4766

    M, W, A—better to designer contemporary apparel

23. Phyllis Wiener
    32 Gramercy Park South
    Phone: 212-475-6425

    W, A—*"fashion advisor to contemporary, upscale stores:* sportswear, dresses, *lingerie, shoes,* and *handbags"*

24. *Retail Consulting Service*
    460 West 34th St.
    Phone: 212-239-1100

    M, W, C

25. *Robin Gruber*
    50 West 77th St.
    Phone: 212-580-9450

    W—complete women's apparel

26. *Rochelle Bergian Bridal Buying*
    1385 Broadway
    Phone: 212-382-2224

    Specializing in moderate to better bridal—*full-service consultations*

27. Sheila Frischman Assoc.
    300 East 40th St.
    Phone: 212-490-3196

    M, W, C, A

28. Sophisticated Buys
    1411 Broadway
    Phone: 212-819-9080

    W sportswear, M off-price sportswear

29. Sunrise Buying
    450 Seventh Ave.
    Phone: 212-594-0170

    M, W—from jrs. to plus and large sizes—off-price

30. Think Big Buys
    110 West 40th St.
    Phone: 212-221-1085

    W—*large* sizes for *specialty stores,* off-price misses sportswear, *"individual approach"*

31. Values At Large
    2 Charleton St.
    Phone: 212-741-3695

    W—*plus* sizes: dresses, sportswear, outerwear

32. Vicki Ross
    32 East 38th St.
    Phone: 212-889-5426

    W, A—*specialized complete consultant* for *specialty stores with exclusive women's clientele: designer* RTW, *cosmetics*, and *decorative home furnishings*

33. Wayne Starr Assoc.
    352 Seventh Ave.
    Phone: 212-736-4155

    M, W—"Specialize in *fur and leather* apparel"

34. Wiener Poller Buying Service
    505 Eighth Ave.
    Phone: 212-279-3388

    M, B, W, G, A—jrs.—petites, large sizes

Los Angeles

BUYING OFFICE	CATEGORIES AND SIZES
1. Apparel Buyers Services 3518 Cahuenga West Phone: 323-436-0236	
2. Directives West 110 East Ninth St. Phone: 213-627-5921	M, W, C, A
3. Marshall Kline Buying Service	W—complete: jrs., misses, petites, women and plus

112 West 9th St.
Phone: 213-689-1269

sizes—including *uniforms*—budget, moderate to upper gifts, gourmet & home furnishings

Dallas

BUYING OFFICE	CATEGORIES AND SIZES
1. Billye Little & Assoc. 3500 Stemmons Freeway Phone: 214-634-0691	M, A—sportswear, *leather, suede* furnishings, *headwear B-8-20 urban* contemporary

The following is a list of several other buying offices to give you an idea of how they charge. They cannot, of course, quote what your fee schedule might be because they would need to know the particulars of your business—and only a shop that has been in business for more than a year can supply that. They can, however, quote you a start-up fee, depending on what services you need or want.

New York Buying Offices:

1. Carol Hoffman Buying Office: Fees depend on type and number of shops or stores (hereafter referred to as "S&S" or "S or S"). "It depends on what services a S or S is looking for: services range from newsletter information to handholding" (which means the buyer accompanies the client into the market to do the actual buying with the client).
2. Phyllis Wiener: Monthly fee. "I send a 400–500 page report, after each of the four or five trade shows a year, to clients that contains *every* bit of information, *every item* they need for buying. All my clients have to do is fill in

sizes they want to order—everything, every single thing else is done for the account."

3. Rochelle Bergian Bridal Buying: Monthly fee. "We are the *only bridal buying office* left in New York. We won't *take* orders if we think delivery will be delayed."

4. Fashion Express: Monthly fee according to size, how many S or S, and volume. "Some offices charge S & S by volume, some by commission. But we feel the most equitable way is monthly. We pride ourselves in giving the best service and information available as possible for that fee."

5. Herbert Gluckson Buying Service: "Fees are negotiable."

6. Lady Budd Affiliates Lba Buying: "Fees are based on gross volume."

7. Vicki Ross: "A monthly fee involves the number of categories or departments an account wants included. But there are two other ways fees are computed: one is an hourly fee just for advice; the other is on a project basis that involves a beginning and an end." Such a project could be, for instance, for a start-up business.

8. Think Big Buys: "Based on a flat monthly fee for a one or two S or S operation."

9. Wiener Poller Buying Service: This is a commission office, which is *free* to S & S. Manufacturers pay a commission to the buying service.

10. Dis Outfitters: A schedule of fees based on annual volume.

11. Fashion Connection: Monthly fee based on the number of S or S.

Los Angeles Buying Offices:

1. Directives West: Fee depends on the type, sizes, and what information is required.

2. Marshall Kline Buying Service: An annual retainer based on a monthly fee.

Dallas Buying Office:

1. Billye Little & Associates: "There are two methods of payment. One is a one-time fee for opening a shop; the other is a monthly fee for ongoing service."

E-Commerce Sites

Here are some websites that can help you in your e-commerce enterprise.

www.allbusiness.com

www.americanexpress.com

www.clickandbuild.com

www.cnctek.com

www.discovercard.com

www.ecommerceinternational.net

www.ffward.com

www.importexporthelp.com/internetmarketing01.htm

www.insideid.com

www.lexiconn.com

www.mastercard.com

www.merchantselect.com

www.networkcomputing.com

www.networksolutions.com

www.verisign.com

www.visa.com

www.websitemarketingplan.com

www.worldpay.com

Resource Guide to the Success Stories

Here is the contact information for the shops and consultants profiled in this book.

The Carmel Hat Company
Doud Arcade
Ocean Ave. between San Carlos &
 Dolores
Carmel, CA 93923
Phone: 831-625-9510

Velo Pro & Trailhead
633 State Street
Santa Barbara, CA 93101
Phone: 805-963-7775
Fax: 805-963-4818
www.velopro.com

Why Not
200 King Street
Alexandria, VA. 22314
Phone: 703-548-4420

Gaspar Cardinale
P.O. Box 2357
Carmel, CA 93921

Coffee and The Works
1627 Connecticut Avenue, N.W.
Washington, D.C. 20009
Phone: 202-483-8050
Fax: 202-483-7030

Jan de Luz
Dolores bet. Ocean & 7th
P.O. Box 1115
Carmel, CA 93921
Phone: 831-622-7621
Fax: 831-622-7250
www.jandeluz.com

Helia's
1338 Wisconsin Ave., N.W.
Georgetown
Washington, D.C. 20007
Phone: 202-333-1241
Fax: 202-333-1251

Henning's
28 West Figueroa Street
Santa Barbara, CA 93101
Phone: 805-965-6107
Toll Free: 888-293-CAKE
Fax: 805-962-3994
www.henningscake.com

West Hartford Professional Family Hair Care
18 La Salle Road
West Hartford, CT 06107

The Book Den
15 East Anapamu Street
Santa Barbara, CA 93101
Phone: 805-962-3321
Fax: 805-965-2844
E-mail: webmail@bookden.com
www.bookden.com

Landis General Store
138–142 N. Larchmont Blvd.
Los Angeles, CA 90004
Phone: 323-465-7998
Fax: 323-465-8143
E-mail:
    info@landisgeneralstore.com

Husk
Shop Address:
176 Collins Street
Melbourne, Victoria 3000
AUSTRALIA

3–13 William St.
Balaclava, Victoria 3183
AUSTRALIA
Phone: + 613-9528-7411
Fax: + 613-9528-7466
E-mail:
    justinabrahams@husk.com.au
www.husk.com.au

Buosi
San Marco 5382/1
30124 Venice
ITALY
Phone & Fax: + 041-520-8567

L'Atelier
1202-A Montana Ave.
Santa Monica, CA 90403
Phone: 310-394-4665
Fax: 310-394-0495
www.latelier.com

Felloni
Via Canonica, 6
44100 Ferrara
ITALY
Phone: +0532-209509

The Tea House
24 Neal St., Covent Garden
London, WC2H 9QW
ENGLAND
Phone: +44 (0) 20-7240-2128
Fax: +44 (0) 20-7836-8273

Papier Mâché
Calle Lunga S. Maria Formosa
   5175
Venice
ITALY
Phone & Fax: +041-522-9995
E-mail:
   papiermache@papiermache.it
www.papiermache.it

Juel
118–122 Queen St.
Queens Court
Woollahra, NSW 2025
AUSTRALIA
Phone: +2-9362-1898
Fax: +2-9818-1898
enquiries@juel.com.au
www.juel.com.au

La Conversation
638 N. Doheny Dr.
West Hollywood, CA 90069
Phone: 310-858-0950
Fax: 310-275-2605

Bella and Daisy's
1750 Union Street
San Francisco, CA 94123
Phone: 415-440-7007
Fax: 415-440-7008
www.bellaanddaisys.com

KRML
The Eastwood Building
San Carlos & 5th
P.O. Box 7300
Carmel, CA 93921
Phone: 831-624-6431
E-mail:david@krml.com
www.krmlradio.com

The Pilgrim's Way Bookstore
and Garden Shop
Dolores bet. 5th & 6th
P.O. Box 1944
Carmel, CA 93921
Phone: 831-624-4955 or 800-
549-9922
E-mail:pilgrim@pilgrimsway.com
www.pilgrimsway.com

Cottage of Sweets
Ocean Avenue
bet. Lincoln & Monte Verde
P.O. Box 5935
Carmel, CA 93921
Phone: 831-624-5170
Fax: 800-620-0106
www.cottageofsweets.com

Candlesticks of Carmel
Ocean at Monte Verde
P.O. Box 6355
Carmel, CA 93921
Phone: 831-626-4305
E-mail:
info@candlesticksofcarmel.com
www.candlesticksofcarmel.com

Nature's Bounty By-The-Sea
Lincoln bet. Ocean & 7th
P.O. Box 2633
Carmel, CA 93921
Phone: 831-626-0920
Fax: 831-625-1433
E-mail:
naturesbounty@nbgems.com
www.nbgems.com

Tiger Lilly Florist
7th bet. San Carlos & Mission
P.O. Box 253
Carmel, CA 93921
Phone: 831-625-1029 or 800-
992-5455
Fax: 831-625-2129

Redeem
Mission bet. 5th & 6th
P.O. Box 833
Carmel, CA 93921
Phone: 831-622-9645

Whittaker's
Ocean near Dolores
P.O. Box 248
Carmel, CA 93921
Phone: 831.624.2185

Bittner

Ocean Avenue

P.O. Box 1402

Carmel, CA 93921

Phone: 888-248-8637

          831-626-3828

Fax: 831.626.8810

E-mail: detlef@bittner.com

www.bittner.com

Carmel Doll Shop

Lincoln & 5th

P.O. Box 7198

Carmel, CA 93921

Phone: 831-625-5360

Fax: 831-625-1433

E-mail: Michaelndavid@

   carmeldollshop.com

www.carmeldollshop.com

Hollie Davies

HTD Marketing

E-mail: hollywudus@yahoo.com

Every Little Thing

Doud Craft Studios

Doud Arcade

bet. Ocean & 7th

P.O. Box 4055

Carmel, CA 93921

Phone: 831-625-1723

Fax: 831-624-4298

E-mail: eltcarmelca@aol.com

Index

Abrahams, Justin, 114
accountant, hiring, 83
accounting, in SCORE symposium, 78
Actis Grande Assoc., 200
active partners, 80
activities, *see* events
advertising, 127–128
  cable TV, 132–133
  direct mail, 117
  editorials for, 161
  e-mail, 148–149
  movie complexes, 133–134
  newspaper, 129–130
  special-interest publications, 130–131, 156
  word-of-mouth, 41, 44, 48, 64, 91, 118, 122, 170
  yellow pages, 95, 124, 133
advertising agency, full-service, 128–129
Alberta Gift Show, 188, 190
Alexandria, Virginia, Why Not, 26–27, 72, 211

ambience, 23–24
  and displays, 35
  theme and, 26–28
antique shop, pricing in, 87
antiques, for display, 73
AOL, 137
apothecary cabinet, 73
apparel, 10–11
  purchasing, 58
  trade shows for buyers, 14–15, 191–198
Apparel Buyers Services, 205
apprentices of mask making, 47
Arnold, Tegan, 159–162
art galleries, 20–21, 55
Aspen, Colorado, 34
L'Atelier (yarn shop), 154–157, 213
Atlanta Gift Fair, 188, 190
attitude of sales personnel, 103–104
Aylaian, Willa, 20–21

bakery, French, 35–40
balloons, 183

bank loans, 80
Barbara Fields Buying Office, 201
barber shop, 29
Barthel, Dan, 64
Barzilay Goldberg Buying Office, 201
Bella and Daisy's (dog bakery), 166–171, 213
Beverly's Best Buys, 201
Big Lots Buying Office, 201
Billye Little & Assoc., 206
    fees, 208
Bittner, Detlef, 60–61
Bittner—The Pleasure of Writing, 61, 215
Blueprints plan, 31–33
Bonometto, Riccardo, 40–42
Book Den, 151–154, 212
books, 9
    Pilgrim's Way, 163–166, 214
    Thunderbird Bookstore, 171–174
Boston Gift Show, 13, 189, 191
    museum reproductions, 9
bridal shop grand opening, 183–184
Bruhn, Leslie, 59–60
budget, 67
bulletin board, local event promotions, 165
Buosi, 40–42, 213
Burke, Tom, 80–81
business financing, in SCORE symposium, 78
business license, 82
business plan, 79–80
Butler Buying Service, 201
buyers, apparel trade shows for, 14–15, 191–198
buying offices, 198–208
    fees, 199–200, 206
    list of, 200–206
    value of membership, 199
buying philosophy, 68
buying plan, 81

cable TV advertising, 132–133
cake shop, 92–96
California Gift Show, 187
Camden, Michelle, 120–123
Canadas, Michael, 158–159
Candlesticks of Carmel, 59–60, 214
Cardinale, Gaspar, 84–88, 211
Carmel, California, 52–55
    Bittner—The Pleasure of Writing, 61, 215
    Candlesticks of Carmel, 59–60, 214
    Carmel Doll Shop, 157–159, 215
    Carmel Hat Company, 89–92, 211
    Cottage of Sweets, 61–63, 214
    Every Little Thing, 20, 215
    Jan de Luz, 43–45, 212
    KRML, 74–76, 213
    Nature's Bounty by the Sea, 64, 214
    Pilgrim's Way, 163–166, 214
    Redeem, 27, 214
    Tiger Lilly Florist, 30, 214
    Whittaker's, 20–21, 214
Carmel Doll Shop, 157–159, 215
Carmel Hat Company, 89–92, 211
Carmona, Michael, 36
Carnivale, 46, 47
Carol Hoffman Buying Office, 201
    fees, 206
Carson, Steve, 36

categories of shops, 6–8
catering, for grand opening, 181
celebrity, at grand opening, 183
Chaine, Séraphie, 147–151
charge accounts, 86
charities
  auctions, 161
  gift basket donation, 170
  involvement in, 145, 175–176
children, 48
children's market, 14–15, 72
  trade shows for buyers, 195
Christmas-in-July event, 143
clientele, 41
clothing, *see* apparel
Coffee and the Works, 120–123, 211
collectibles, 20
color themes, 27
community service, 143, 174, 175
computer software, for inventory control, 81
La Conversation, 35–40, 213
co-op websites, 135
cost estimates, 15–16
Cottage of Sweets, 61–63, 214
creativity, 19
credit card companies, e-commerce information from, 136–137
credit cards, 86
credit union loans, 80
Cruz, Graciela, 38
Cruz, Nubia, 38
Custom Buying Service, 201
customer appreciation day, 143
customer relations, 47
customer service, 45, 69, 91, 97
  training staff on, 111–113
customers
  avoiding quick judgment, 42, 120

dissatisfied, 101
factors impacting purchase by, 88
garden for attracting, 29
input from, 44
niche type appealing to, 50–51
replenishable, 90–91
salespersons' interaction with, 57
customized logos, 142

Dallas International Gift and Home Accessories Market, 188, 189, 190, 191
Damskey, Karen, 154
Danskin, 8
Davies, Hollie, 127
Davis, Hollie, 215
Debagamage, Kamal, 96n
demographics, 50
Denise Minsky Buying Group, 202
department stores, 11
Dianne Cohan Assoc., 202
direct mail advertising, 117
Directives West, 205
  fees, 207
Dis Outfitters, 202
  fees, 207
discount coupons, 179
discounts, 24
display windows, 34–35, 44
  changing, 116
  for shock effect, 184–185
displays, 30–33
  and ambience, 35
  frequency for changing, 109
  at grand opening, 178
  importance, 30
  for jewelry, 160
  types, 25–26

dissatisfied customers, 101
dog bakery, 166–171
downloading forms from SCORE, 15–16
downtime, training on use, 109

East Coast Show, 188
Eastwood, Clint, 53, 74
e-commerce, 88, 135–136
  websites, 209
editorials, for advertising, 161
education, 99
e-mail, 134
  for advertising, 148–149
  for promotions, 139
embroidery machine, 43–44
employees, 94
  learning from, 106–109
  "Personnel Incentives Program," 115–116
  see also sales personnel
entertainment, at grand opening, 178–179
Evans, Joanne, 203
evening shopping, conditions for, 51
events
  advertising, 144–145
  in-store, 24, 165
Every Little Thing, 20, 215
Excelsior Fashion Inc., 202
excuses, 95
expansion of business, 53
expiration date on coupons, 179
exterior décor, 28–30

fabric shop, 117–120
Facchin, Elfriede, 147–151
fads, 68
"fall back" fund, 67

Fashion Connection Buying Office, 202
  fees, 207
Fashion Express, 202
  fees, 207
feature articles, 141–142
federal income taxes, 82
fees, of buying offices, 206
Felloni, 117–120, 213
Felloni, Alberto, 117–120
Felloni, Giulio, 117–120
Fernandes, Cynthia, 164
Ferrara, Italy, Felloni, 117–120, 213
Fictitious Business Name petition, 82
finances
  budget, 67
  cost estimates, 15–16
  level needed, 84
  SCORE advice on, 77–81
  for startup, 60, 148
financial planning, 15–16
flyers, 140–141
foot traffic, 51, 62, 76
  location and, 58
forms, downloading from SCORE, 15–16
French bakery, 35–40
Frére, Edie, 9
Fridlund, Paul, 163–166
friendship, 47
full-service advertising agency, 128–129
funding sources, 80
furnishings, 10–11
furniture shop, vs. furniture store, 10–11

Gabe Mozarsky Co., 202
garden, as customer attraction, 29

The Gazebo, 24, 35
Geneva, Switzerland, 55
Georgetown, Washington, D.C.,
    Helia's, 56–59, 212
gift fairs, 11–15
gift shows, 71
gift wrapping, 73, 145
giveaways at grand opening, 179
Golden Rule of retailing, 9–10, 98
Goldhirsch Group, Inc., 84
Google, 137
Gottardo, Eliana, 46
Gottardo, Manuela, 46
Gottardo, Stefano, 46
grand opening, 175
    of bridal shop, 183–184
    displays, 178
    entertainment, 178–179
    giveaways, 179
    guest book, 181–182
    invitations to, 176–177
    newsworthiness, 182–183
    prizes, 179
    promoting, 182–183
    refreshments, 181
gross receipts taxes, 83
Gruber, Robin, 204
guest book, at grand opening,
    181–182

Harry Potter books, 61
Helia's, 56–59, 212
Henning's (cake shop), 92–96,
    212
Herbert J. Gluckson Buying Ser-
    vice, 203
    fees, 207
Hermes shops, 27–28
Heydari, Mariam, 57
hiring sales personnel, 101–104
hobby, retailing as, 100

home furnishings, 11
honesty, 95
Husk, 113–117, 212

income taxes, 82
in-store events, 165
in-store promotions, 144
insurance, 82
interior décor, 25–26
    Blueprints plan, 31–33
interior displays, 90
    changing, 116
Internet sales, 51, 64, see also
    e-commerce
inventory
    level for startup, 85
    storage, 90
inventory control system, 57, 81
invitations to grand opening,
    176–177

Jagger, Mick, 59
Jan de Luz, 43–45, 212
Jane Tucker Enterprises, 203
jewelry, 159–162
job interview, 103
Johnson, Seward, 34
Juel, 159–162, 213
J.W. Merchandising, 203

Kelley, Eric, 151–154
Kim, Jane Bok, 30n
Kimball, David, 74
Kjar, Wayne, 92–96
KRML, 74–76, 213

Lady Budd Affiliates Lba Buying,
    203
    fees, 207
Landis General Store, 9, 65–71,
    212

Las Vegas, 34
legal matters, in SCORE symposium, 78
liability insurance, 82
licenses, 82
limited partners, 80
line of bank credit, 84
linen shop, 43
listening, 91–92, 95
local event promotions, bulletin board for, 165
location, 41, 49, 94–95
    foot traffic and, 58
    longevity factors of, 51
    recognizing undesirable, 52
logos
    on business promotional items, 179
    customized, 142
London, Tea House, 17–19, 213
Los Angeles Fashion, Gift & Home Market, 189
Los Angeles Gift & Home Market Show, 190, 191
Los Angeles: Hancock Park, 66
Los Angeles, Landis General Store, 9, 65–71, 212
Luplus, Brigitte, 43

maps of tourist areas, 62
markdowns, timing of, 87
market research, SCORE workshop on, 78
marketing
    budget, 146
    defining, 127–129
    word-of-mouth as best, 146
    see also advertising; public relations (PR)
markup, formulas for, 86–87

Marshall Kline Buying Service, 205–206
    fees, 208
Martin Bayer Assoc., 203
mask shop, 45–48
McMahon, Elsa, 159–162
media buyers, 128
Medicare taxes, 82
Melbourne, Australia, Husk, 113–117, 212
Men's Night, 24
men's shop, 40–42
menswear
    shows for, 14
    trade shows for buyers, 195–196
merchandise
    donating to charities, 145
    in mini-boutiques, 69
merchandise display, 30–33
Mi & Canna, 147
mini-boutiques, 65
Montreal Gift Show, 189, 191
Morsdome, Kyong, 30
movie complexes, local merchant advertising, 133–134

national magazines, advertising in, 132
National Stationery Show, 190
Nature's Bounty by the Sea, 214
New York Cash & Carry . . . Gifts to Go Show, 189
New York Extracts Show, 189
New York Home Textiles Show, 189, 191
New York International Contemporary Furniture Fair, 189
New York International Gift Fair (NYIGF), 12–13, 187–188, 190

New York trade shows, museum reproductions, 9
newsletters, 138–139
newspaper advertising, 129–130
newsworthiness, of grand opening, 182–183
niche business, 4
    benefits of owning, 5
    finding, 6–9
    shops within shops, 65
    uniqueness, 49
    what it is, 5
notebook, for planning, 10
The No. 1 Ladies' Detective Agency (Smith), 18
Nunez, Rick, 64

O'Daniel, Frank, 171*n*
open-to-buy (OTB), 81
Orlando Gift Show, 188, 190
O'Shea, Veronica, 27
owners, *see* shop owners
owning niche shop, benefits of, 5

paid advertising, *see* advertising
Papier Mâché, 45–48, 213
Paris, Scabass, 147–151
parking, 95
    need for, 51
partners, 80
part-time retail shop, 100
permits, 82
personal buying service, 69
"Personnel Incentives Program," 115–116
phone books for advertising, 95, 124, 133
    for book store, 153
phone calls, training in handling, 104–105

Pilgrim's Way (bookstore), 163–166, 214
planning, 5
    financial, 15–16
    notebook for, 10
Playbill, 145
The Pot Shop, 112–113
press releases, 139–140
Pretty Woman, 120
pricing, 86–87
printer, for grand opening invitations, 176–177
privacy, as e-commerce priority, 137
prizes, 143
    at grand opening, 179
promotions, 142–144
    for grand opening, 182–183
property tax, 83
props for displays, 26
public relations (PR), 128, 138–146
    charity benefits, 145
    customized logos, 142
    e-mail promotions, 139
    feature articles, 141–142
    flyers, 140–141
    gift wrapping, 145
    in-store promotions, 144
    newsletters, 138–139
    press releases, 139–140
    promotions, 142–144
    theater and other event advertising, 144–145
"push money," 60

quality merchandise, 42
QuickBooks software, 44, 81

radio station, 74–76
    demographics, 128

raffles, 179
Reddin, Tom, 29
Redeem, 27, 214
refresher session for training, 110
refreshments at grand opening, 181
regional trade show, 13
Rendondo Beach, California, L'Atelier (yarn shop), 154–157, 213
reputation, 101
Retail Consulting Service, 204
retailing
  primary principles, 98–99
  as right personal fit, 99–101
return policy, 85–86, 91, 94, 110–111
reviewers, of dining facilities, 36–37
Richardson, Kaki, 20
Robinson, David, 158
Rochell Bergian Bridal Buying, 204
  fees, 207
Rooibos, 18
Rose, Lanny, 61–63
Rose, Linda, 61–63
Ross, Vicki, 205
  fees, 207

sales personnel, 74
  attitude of, 103–104
  hiring, 101–104
  interaction with customers, 57
  for jewelry shop, 161
  personalities of, 41
  qualities, 118–119, 124
  value of, 122–123
  see also training of sales personnel
sales representative, 13–14

sales tax, 83
San Diego, California, 55
San Francisco, California, Bella and Daisy's, 166–171, 213
San Francisco Gourmet Products Show, 189
San Francisco International Gift Fair, 188, 190
  museum reproductions, 9
Santa Barbara Book and Author Festival, 153
Santa Barbara, California
  Book Den, 151–154, 212
  gift shop window display, 35
  Henning's (cake shop), 92–96, 212
  Velo Pro and Trailhead, 123–125, 211
Santa Monica, California, L'Atelier (yarn shop), 154–157, 213
Scabass, 147–151
Schlabach, Kate, 26–27, 72
SCORE (Service Corps of Retired Executives), 15–16, 77–81
search engines, 137–138
Seattle Gift Show, 188, 190
"Secret Garden," 164
security, as e-commerce priority, 137
Seres, Carol, 80–81
services for grand opening, exchanging, 178
sfbayshop.com, 135, 170–171
Sheila Frischman Assoc., 204
Shirokow, Susi, 59–60
shop owners
  help from local, 50–51
  involvement, 91
  learning from employee, 106–109

shopping centers, co-op websites, 135
shops
 exterior of, 28–30
 success, 1
showroom, viewing line at, 14
Simmons, Gregor, 202
Small Business Administration (SBA), 15–16
 loans, 80
Small Business Resource Guide, 84
A Small-Business Guide on How to Secure Financing (Goldhirsch Group), 84
Smith, Alexander McCall, The No. 1 Ladies' Detective Agency, 18
Smith, Christina, 17–19
Social Security taxes, 82
Society for the Prevention of Cruelty to Animals, 182–183
Sophisticated Buys, 204
"special event" weekends, 60
special-interest publications, advertising in, 130–131
Springfield, Massachusetts, 34
square foot requirements, for merchandise categories, 31
startup
 advice for, 70
 financial backing for, 60
 inventory needed, 85
 problems in, 71
state income taxes, 82
state license, 82
statistics, on small retail shops, xiii
stock, moving and changing, 34
storage, 32
Stormon, Leslie, 154
street parking, 51
street wear, 148

success
 appearance of, 88
 of shops, 1
Sunrise Buying, 204
suppliers, freebies for grand opening, 179
Sydney, Australia, Juel, 159–162, 215

"target" audience, for advertising, 130–131
taxes, 82–83
Tea House, 17–19, 213
theater advertising, 144–145
theme, 26–28, 103, 149
 color, 27
Think Big Buys, 204
 fees, 207
3—13 William St., 212
Thunderbird Bookstore, 171–174
Tiffany's Table Manners for Teenagers, 9
Tiger Lilly Florist, 30, 214
timing
 for buying, 69
 of markdowns, 87
 for selling, 9–10
Toronto International Gift Fair, 188
tourist areas, 51
 in Carmel, California, 53
 niche categories, 9
 Web page for business in, 134
tourist map, 62
trade organizations, 198
trade shows, 11–15, 187–198
Trailhead, 123–125, 211
training of sales personnel, 99, 104–106, 116
 on customer service, 111–113
 on downtime use, 109

trends, clues for, 70–71
turnover rate, 1
turns, 69–70, 85
TV channel audience, 128

U.S. Census Bureau, xiii
U.S. Patent and Trademark Office, 82

Values At Large, 205
Vancouver Gift Show, 189
Velo Pro and Trailhead, 123–125, 211
vendors, freebies for grand opening, 179
Venice, Italy
    Buosi, 40–42, 213
    Papier Mâché, 45–48, 213
Very Last Day Sale, 24
vignettes, 33–34
volunteers in SCORE, 78

Waldroup, Mary, 171
Washington, D.C.
    Coffee and the Works, 120–123, 211
    Helia's, 56–59, 212
Washington, D.C. Gift Show, 188, 190
Wayne Starr Assoc., 205
Web page templates, 137
website developers, 134
websites, 88, 134–138
    for Bella and Daisy's, 170–171

for Book Den, 152
co-op, 135
e-commerce, 209
for trade shows, 13, 15
weekends, "special event," 60
West Hartford Professional Family Hair Care, 29, 212
West Hollywood, California, La Conversation, 35–40, 215
Whittaker's, 20–21, 214
Why Not, 26–27, 72, 211
Wiener, Phyllis, 204
    fees, 206–207
Wiener Poller Buying Service, 205
    fees, 207
window displays, 34–35, 44
    changing, 116
    for shock effect, 184–185
Windsor, England, 55
womenswear trade shows, 14, 191–193, 197–198
word-of-mouth advertising, 41, 44, 48, 64, 91, 118, 122, 170
worker's compensation, 82

Yahoo, 137
"Yappie Hour," 170
yellow pages, 95, 124, 133
    for book store advertising, 153

Zajiakhami, Omid, 57
zoning requirements, 82